GALVANIZED

GALVANIZED

The Odyssey of a Reluctant
Carolina Confederate

MICHAEL K. BRANTLEY

Potomac Books

AN IMPRINT OF THE UNIVERSITY OF NEBRASKA PRESS

© 2020 by Michael K. Brantley

All rights reserved. Potomac Books is an imprint of the
University of Nebraska Press.
Manufactured in the United States of America.

♾

Library of Congress Cataloging-in-Publication Data
Names: Brantley, Michael K., author.
Title: Galvanized: the odyssey of a reluctant Carolina
Confederate / Michael K. Brantley.
Other titles: Odyssey of a reluctant Carolina Confederate
Description: Lincoln, NE: Potomac Books, an imprint of the
University of Nebraska Press, [2020] | Includes bibliographical
references.
Identifiers: LCCN 2019031715
ISBN 9781640121225 (hardback)
ISBN 9781640123144 (epub)
ISBN 9781640123151 (mobi)
ISBN 9781640123168 (pdf)
Subjects: LCSH: Batchelor, Wright Stephen, 1828–1886.
| Soldiers—Confederate States of America—Biography. |
Confederate States of America. Army. North Carolina Infantry
Regiment, 47th—Biography. | United States. Army. Volunteer
Infantry Regiment, 1st—Biography. | Prisoners of war—
United States—Biography. | Prisoners of war—Confederate
States of America—Biography. | Point Lookout Prison Camp
for Confederates—Biography. | United States—History—Civil
War, 1861–1865—Prisoners and prisons. | United States—
History—Civil War, 1861–1865—Biography. | Murder victims—
North Carolina—Nash County—Biography.
Classification: LCC E546.4 .B73 2020 | DDC 973.7/42092
[B]—dc23
LC record available at https://lccn.loc.gov/2019031715

Set in Scala OT by Laura Ebbeka.

For my favorite historian, Kristi

Contents

Illustrations

Acknowledgments

It is remarkable how many people it takes to create a book—it only begins with the author. I loved every minute of working on *Galvanized*, but it never would have come to pass without a host of others, to whom I am grateful beyond measure.

That starts with the fine folks at Potomac Books/University of Nebraska Press. Tom Swanson believed in the book and me early on and was encouraging all the way, always keeping me informed. Abigail Stryker is a patient woman, as she worked to gather all the details and essentials. Sara Springsteen, the project editor, kept this book organized and on schedule, and Jane Curran offered diligent and thorough editing to improve the final product. Roger Buchholz exceeded any expectations I could have imagined for the cover art. Tish Fobben helped it look and sound its best on the cover and in catalogs.

Research sometimes seems never-ending, and it can be on a project like this. Librarians can be a writer's best friend, and I owe a debt to Traci Thompson from Braswell Library in Rocky Mount, North Carolina; Shirlyn, Ian, Grace, and Chip at the North Carolina Wesleyan College Library; Robert Anthony and the folks at the North Carolina Collection and Wilson Library at UNC–Chapel Hill; the staff at the North Carolina State Archives and others at the North Carolina Department of Cultural Resources; and the Wilson County Public Library, as well as the fine people at Broadfoot Publishing's bookstore, especially Tom Broadfoot.

I'm grateful to those who read and offered comments on *Galva-*

nized, a group of wonderful and generous writers: Wade Dudley, Philip Gerard, Rebecca McClanahan, and Jon Pineda. There is also a special place in my heart for all those who researched, recorded, and protected the history of this country over the last two centuries. They are underappreciated.

Finally, I owe many thanks to my family for their help and support, especially my wife, Kristi, who tracked down many elusive elements and is always my first reader, and my daughter, Holly, who assisted on more than one "field trip." I appreciate my boys, Kent and Lowell, who sacrificed time at play and gave me space when I needed to crank out pages.

Introduction

The Civil War is our felt history—history
lived in the national imagination.

—ROBERT PENN WARREN, *Legacy of the Civil War*

It is well that war is so terrible, otherwise
we should grow too fond of it.

—Gen. ROBERT E. LEE to Gen. James Longstreet

There are not many accounts of the Civil War from the viewpoint of the men in the ranks. There is the incredibly well written *Company Aytch* by Sam R. Watkins of the First Tennessee Infantry, Company H, but most of the memoirs are from the viewpoints of officers or well-known figures.

There are four main reasons for this.

1. There was not much literacy during this time period in the South or the North, but public education in the South in particular was poor.

2. The common men did not paint a glorious picture or speak of a majestic, mythical "Lost Cause." The men who served on the front line rarely offered propaganda or romantic notions.

3. In North Carolina in particular, there was not much of an appetite for war.

4. The privates and "regular" people saw and lived the brutal reality of a civil war.

This book is meant to offer a history, a personal story, and a plea to look at this era in American history from other viewpoints, to move the camera from its fixed position, perhaps around to the side. There is rarely a time or place or situation, particularly in regard to history, where people would not benefit from such a consideration.

The story of the common person is often the one that goes untold. However, because of that limited supply, it can at times be interesting, and certainly more humanizing, than combat reports. It is hard to imagine what else could be written about the famous characters of the war. But how about the non-household names? How do we not know these stories? We thought as schoolchildren, at least I did, that history was written and recorded, but whatever we studied was only part of the story. A step back from our evolved selves, equipped with perfect hindsight, to consider what choices you might have had if you were a poor farmer in the era of 1861–65, will offer new considerations. The rich aristocratic men who started the war can be held accountable for sins of slavery; as is usually the case, they weren't the ones who did the dying. History is never really truly and completely presented, only partially so, and even then, so much of it is lost. Local history is important, argu-ably more so than the well-known, well-organized facts in text-books. It connects and offers identity to communities and makes our past more understandable and relatable. History doesn't seem so far removed when the stories aren't about icons but about real people. This history is often more truthful and more interesting.

The Civil War is not an either/or moment in history—it was a complex and complicated and tangled time, as were the people involved—and it is almost impossible to give short explanations or untangle their beliefs and thoughts and actions. What I thought I knew was met with many turns, and my ideas about the war shifted numerous times while researching this book. This time period was the most knotted time in the history of this great country. One thing is clear—we should all thank God the South lost. The Civil War was the biggest waste of life in our history, and it might have ended slavery, but it did not free the black man.

What is written here is in no way meant to glorify the war, or one man or any men. It is meant to show the struggle and the conflict, not just in the field but in the conscience and in the morals of the people of America in the middle of the nineteenth century, a time full of contradictions. It illustrates that history, and the men and women who made it, were imperfect. It is complicated beyond belief, and time has not made it less so.

While I am no apologist, I do think the South in general and North Carolina in particular have to be viewed from a unique viewpoint. As a native Tar Heel, I hope I'm allowed that bias.

There is a lot of corruption in the view of the Civil War by those living a century and a half later. There are a lot of half-truths, untruths, stereotypes, assumptions, and general misunderstanding. Presentism is part of the problem, of course. The thinking during this time, less than one hundred years into the formation of the country, was still regional. There had been secession talk during the War of 1812 and before, and there certainly was not strong unity among the colonies during the American Revolution.

The war and its aftermath were the low point in America's history, the evidence of which is the pain still faced today regarding the figures and symbols and the controversies surrounding them.

The research that went into this book sometimes solidified my thoughts on the Civil War, sometimes shifted them, but most often conflicted them even more. I'm surprised at my views on flags, monuments, people, and attitudes, and scared at how much many of us think we know until we look up a topic for ourselves.

Study and broad reading of the American Civil War at once produces sadness, anger, and wonder at the waste of life and treasure, all of which should have been avoided. That it was not reveals the worst of the character of the time. The fact that the nation reunified and persevered reveals the best.

When we will recover from that war is up for debate.

GALVANIZED

I

Homecoming

The Civil War defined us as what we are and it opened us to being what we became, good and bad things. . . . It was the crossroads of our being, and it was a hell of a crossroads.

—SHELBY FOOTE, historian and author

The man straggling down the dusty, eastern North Carolina dirt road was dark and dirty and wore tattered clothes—a threadbare shirt, worn gray trousers, and shoes coming apart at the seams. It was an exceptionally warm day for early spring, and he was hot. Black matted hair jutted from his head in all directions under a kepi cap, blending into a ratty beard that hung nearly to his chest. He was beanpole thin, and his shoulders drooped; his eyes were sunken with heavy dark circles underneath. He looked wild, feral, hollow.

Sally Ann, a plain but pretty woman in her thirties, was preparing to call her children from the fields for a midday meal and had to stop and take a long look. Was this an outlaw, someone who might do them harm? In the last months of the war, and since it ended, reports of roving bands of marauders were not uncommon. The location of her husband's shotgun slipped through her thoughts quickly. In the chaos and desperation of the current state of affairs, she had to be constantly vigilant for robbers, scoundrels, and desperados. Word was that Robert E. Lee had surrendered in Virginia, but the war continued, and that devil Bill Sherman was in North Carolina, camped at the state capital, Raleigh. She'd heard nothing of her beloved and wasn't even sure if he was still alive; she'd heard little more than rumors of his whereabouts. Suddenly, she recognized the gait as one she hadn't seen in three years. The stranger was her husband, alive, in one piece. A blessing. Sally Ann pulled at her skirt hem and broke into a trot toward him, calling out through tears of jubilation and disbelief.

But the physical reunion would have to wait. The man raised his arms. "Stop right there," he yelled. "Don't come no closer. I'm eat up with all kinds of mess."

Exhausted, weary, hungry, and defeated, he instructed his wife to fill up a tub of water in the yard and to keep the young'uns away, lest he infest them all with the lice and filth that consumed him. Sally Ann nodded and turned back to run to the house, calling to her oldest four children, who had all gathered on the porch, to help her. They were startled by the commotion over the man they were just now beginning to recognize, something they could hardly believe. The children could barely contain themselves as they hauled buckets of water and dumped it into the old washtub.

"Daddy! Daddy!" they shouted over and over. The man, five feet seven with brown-black eyes and sun-worn, leathery features, was excited to see his family, but he was done in and looked older than his years. The two youngest children, barely knee-high, stared at the spectacle, wondering who the stranger was, and how anyone so filthy could strip off all his clothes in the yard and not be yelled at or run off by their mama.

Wright Stephen Batchelor was finally home from the Civil War. He had walked 135 miles from Appomattox Courthouse in Virginia since April 9, 1865, all the way to the outskirts of Nashville, a rural county seat town in Nash County, North Carolina. Once he had drowned all the lice, his wife burned his clothes and brought him some of his old things to wear, which hung on him like a scarecrow.

He had seen some things many men chose not to talk about. He'd survived horrors unimaginable, death, disease, and destruction, and all the in-between, the worst of human suffering. Misery had been his constant companion over the previous year and a half. He'd tramped all over North Carolina, Virginia, Maryland, and

Pennsylvania, woods and swamps and rivers and creek beds and fields, even to the Midwest frontier and back to near the present-day communities of White Oak and Momeyer. He'd faced hurricanes of grape and canister, and incoming rifle fire that filled the air like swarms of bees. He'd run at the enemy, away from the enemy, and hidden from both friend and foe as circumstances required, although telling one from the other was often difficult. If nothing else, Wright was a survivor, no easy task that year.

Even for a grizzled Confederate veteran who had spent weeks navigating roads, rivers, woods, and human hazards after three years of war, that meeting on the porch was emotionally overwhelming. Wright, 36, had never laid eyes on his youngest child, Fannie, who was born seven months after he left for the army. Sally Ann had barely been showing when he set off for camp. He left their farm early in 1862 and headed west to Fort Mangum in Raleigh, while his wife stayed behind to tend the farm and provide for six children, all under the age of 10 at the time. Now the Batchelors were together again: Eugenia, 12; Lucy Jane, 11; William, 8; Kansas (sometimes called Arkansas), 6; Bunion, 4; and Fannie, 2. In less than a year, Little Sallie Ann would come along, part of the Reconstruction Baby Boom.

While Union troops had not set foot on his remote farm about forty-five miles east of Raleigh, the area had not gone untouched. The cotton mill in nearby Rocky Mount, nineteen miles east, had been burned by a Union force operating out of New Bern in 1863. The Tar River bridge and train depot had been torched as well. No major battles had been fought in this part of the state, but there were plenty of losses to reckon with. Many family members, neighbors, and friends had not yet returned to this farming community, and as time passed it soon became obvious many never would.

Wright's younger brother, Ruffin, hadn't been heard from since he was captured a week earlier on April 3, during the siege and retreat at Petersburg, Virginia. The two were close and had enlisted together in Raleigh, both serving in Company A, the Chicora Guards, of the Forty-Seventh North Carolina Infantry. Later, after Gettys-

3

burg, they were separated when Wright was taken prisoner at the Battle of Bristoe Station in Virginia. Months after his brother's capture, Ruffin transferred to the Thirtieth North Carolina, Company I, where several other relatives and cousins were serving. He was there until he became a POW and was imprisoned at Hart's Island, New York. Ruffin didn't get home until June 1865, nearly two months after the war ended.

Many of Wright's friends and family members did not return at all, scattered instead in makeshift battlefield and prison camp cemeteries. His older brother Vincent, serving in Company A of the Thirty-Third North Carolina, fell to typhus in a Union prisoner of war camp after being captured at Winchester, Virginia. That was just months after signing up as a substitute for another man. He left behind a wife and five children. Death was present on the home front as well, as Wright's older half sister, Pheraby, died while he was gone in 1863. Cousins Merritt, Thomas, John, and William died during the war as well.

Few families went untouched as 125,000 North Carolinians served, the most of any Confederate state. North Carolina supplied more than 10 percent of the entire Confederate Army. Nash County offered 1,427 men, and neighboring Edgecombe sent 1,711.[1]

North Carolina also lost the most men, an estimated 40,000. Half of those losses came in combat, the other half from sickness, disease, and injuries. Another 8,000 Tar Heels (5,000 Colored Troops and 3,000 white soldiers) served in the Union Army.[2] In all, 3.5 million men served on both sides in the War Between the States, and 600,000 died. It was truly our nation's biggest tragedy.

After spending months in the trenches and experiencing tension in the siege of Petersburg, seeing the war unravel, Wright marched out those final days with Gen. Robert E. Lee and the Army of Northern Virginia as they backpedaled and stalled on a retreat that would take them to one last scuffle near the tiny village of Appomattox Courthouse. After Lee and Union general Ulysses S. Grant worked out the details of surrender in Wilmer McLean's front parlor, Lee addressed his men one last time with some advice: "Go back to your homes and resume your occupations. Obey the laws and become as good citizens as you were soldiers."[3]

While Wright's journey might seem like a dramatic scene out of Charles Frazier's acclaimed *Cold Mountain*, it was not an uncommon one for enlisted foot soldiers at the end of the war. It wasn't even his longest or most dangerous trek; in an odd twist, Wright had switched sides in prison and served several months in the Union Army before deserting. He then walked halfway across the country from Wisconsin to Virginia to rejoin his old unit, ducking both Union and Confederate pickets, militia, home guards, and partisan farm families, worried about dangerous and desperate and hungry pillagers, outlaws, and renegades who roamed the back roads and woods all during the war.

Most Confederate infantrymen were poor illiterate farmers before the war, and now with the South devastated, transportation and communication channels were in shambles. Sally Ann had managed to keep the farm going, which along with Wright's work as a superintendent of the county poor house, had supported the family prior to the conflict. Reconstruction hadn't even begun, and rationing and shortages made life difficult. Raging inflation and the now worthless Confederate currency had ruined the South. While Nash County had many free blacks and black landowners before the war, an entire new workforce and class of poor had been created with the Emancipation Proclamation.

But Wright, who never owned slaves, planned to take Lee's advice to heart. While no wealthy planter, he did have a farm to call his own and a growing workforce under his roof, if it was still there. He had been a man of some standing, one who would later be spoken of as "good and clever," not just by his friends and neighbors, but those who knew him by reputation only. He and Sally Ann wasted little time in helping repopulate the South, with Little Sally Ann, Peter Ruffin, Nannie, Jordan, and Wright Jr. coming along in 1866, 1867, 1870, 1872, and 1874, respectively.

While the story of Wright's first day back home has been passed down through his descendants for generations, no one knows what he spoke of first. Not only had he not laid eyes on his wife and children for more than three years, but it appears his family had not heard any of his whereabouts during that time. He was listed as Missing in Action in one state newspaper, but it is not likely the Batchelors at home saw it, and it wouldn't have mattered if they did, as none of them could read or write. A neighbor or shopkeeper perhaps passed on the news. Records show that while he achieved some status in his community, Wright was not literate until the war, according to the 1870 census. No one knows if he made notes of his unlikely odyssey, but he spent a good bit of that time away fighting in most of the major eastern campaigns, dodging minié balls from both Blue and Gray and escaping capture before later serving time in a prison camp, and then running for his life.

He'd had enough adventure, been spared more than once, through luck or Providence or good judgment—perhaps a bit of all three—and was ready to come home to a quiet if hardworking life in the country. His home in the White Oak community was a long way from anywhere, really, somewhat like it is even to this day. Wright was a practical man, like most of those who served in the ranks of the Confederate Army, with no ideology beyond how his pigs and crops would produce in the coming summer.

Wright Stephen Batchelor was my great-great-grandfather, and his unlikely story is one of survival, success, and tragedy. There was a stubbornness about him, a survivor instinct that carried him through the war and got him home in one piece, albeit altered, never to be the same again. In many ways his life was the perfect metaphor for his native state.

2

A Name in a Book

When you spend all day among old papers, the people come alive
for you, and you begin to see the present through different eyes.

—RUTH REICHL, author

On a fall Saturday morning years ago, I was thumbing through a
book at Broadfoot Publishing Company, one of my favorite book-
stores. Located in Wendell, North Carolina, a small town full of
charm about fifteen minutes east of Raleigh and named for poet
Oliver Wendell Holmes Sr., I ran across the following entry, and I
wasn't even looking for it:

BATCHELOR, WRIGHT S.—PRIVATE

Born in Nash County where he resided as a farmer prior to enlist-
ing in Nash County at age 33, February 4, 1862. Captured at Bris-
toe Station, Virginia, October 14, 1863. Confined at Old Capitol
Prison, Washington, D.C. 1863. Transferred to Point Lookout,
Maryland, October 27, 1863. Released at Point Lookout on Febru-
ary 24, 1864, after taking the Oath of Allegiance and joining the
U.S. Army. Assigned to Company F, 1st Regiment, U.S. Volunteer
Infantry. Deserted from Federal service at Milwaukee, Wisconsin,
September 14, 1864. Returned to duty with Company A, 47th Reg-
iment N.C. Troops, on an unspecified date (probably subsequent
to October 31, 1864). Surrendered at Appomattox Court House,
Virginia, April 9, 1865.[1]

I was working with my wife, Kristi, on some genealogy, trying to find details about my Brantley ancestors, and what service they might have had in the Civil War.

Tom Broadfoot opened the store in 1969, and it is the place to go to find the impossible to find, the out of print, and just about anything else related to the Civil War. The store is the "retail" arm of a publisher and collector of volumes that is mind-boggling, and Tom has touched an amazing amount of history in his time. The store is placed inside a nondescript house, near the end of a rural road in Wake County, a place you have to be looking for to find, but once you do, you'll always find your way back. The shelves are set up like stacks in an old library, lined with thousands of volumes, labeled by state in some cases, price in others, and other more specific breakdowns. A shopper can spend from $5 to well into the thousands on any given day of Broadfoot's somewhat peculiar operating hours.

There were entries in the *Roster* for names I recognized—Green, Mack, and Handy Brantley—which were short and to the point. Name, rank, dates of service. I decided to look for other family surnames, since my people are mostly from two eastern North Carolina counties, Nash and Edgecombe, and I ran across a few Batchelors. None of the entries stood out until the one for Wright Stephen Batchelor jumped off the page. First, it was much longer than the others, which was unusual for a private, but when I scanned across the fact he'd been captured, joined the Union Army, deserted, and then, instead of going home, rejoined his old Confederate outfit and finished the war, I thought maybe he was worth checking into. Since I'd never heard his name mentioned by any of my family, I guessed him to be a distant cousin or some other relation, removed a time or two. I was puzzled why no one in my family had ever spoken of him.

With several ancestors in the book, I felt justified in making the $20 purchase, and the book went home and on the shelf, and Wright and the Brantleys, Matthews, Brakes, and others I'd collected got shuffled into a backlog of ideas to take up someday, in some way. The idea did not resurface in a serious manner for more than a decade. After all, Kristi and I were busy running a photography studio and raising three children, and this research was just a hobby. At least it was a hobby until we both went back to graduate school in our forties to pursue passions we'd restrained since college.

Before going back to school and making a career change, I worked for eighteen years as a professional photographer in Nashville, North Carolina, the county seat of Nash County. One day, an old family friend, Terry, came in with some photographs he wanted copied for the local Sons of Confederate Veterans chapter. The Sons of Confederate Veterans was formed in 1896 in Richmond, Virginia, to preserve the memory of all those who served in the Confederate military It is open to male descendants of Confederate veterans who can provide genealogical proof of relation and service (a group for female descendants was started in 1894 in Nashville, Tennessee, the United Daughters of the Confederacy).

Terry's family sold my parents their farm back in the 1950s, the place where I grew up in the 1970s and 1980s and live now in a corner of that original property. This farm is in the southwestern end of the county, about forty miles from Raleigh, five miles from Spring Hope, twelve from Nashville, and twenty from Rocky Mount, the largest city in the county (it actually is in two counties, the other being Edgecombe). Terry is a character, an amateur historian, and a fellow who can spin a yarn that instinctively makes the listener want to disbelieve, but inevitably, upon deeper inspection, his stories usually turn out to be true, or at least mostly so.

For example, he once told me that one of my Brantley ancestors had been a blacksmith in the nearby town of Spring Hope, and that he remembered visiting this shop as a child. Terry is somewhat older than I am, and by my calculations he would have been talking about the 1950s. Even though many farmers were still using mules and horses at that time, I had a hard time believing there would be enough business to keep a blacksmith going. I was dubious, and more so when he told me this: "You know, he's buried over in Oakdale Cemetery, right there in Spring Hope. As a matter of fact, when they buried old Henry, they mounted his anvil and hammer right there on the tombstone."

9

I'm sure my eyebrows lifted as I'd not long ago been to the cemetery for a research project and would not have missed such a distinctive marker. I pressed him for specific locations, and as he sometimes tends to be, he was "vaguely specific," mentioning the back of the burying ground as if it was the size of a backyard, when in reality it is several shaded acres near the railroad tracks in a section of town that still features some unpaved streets. I went back to Oakdale before the week was over, parked and walked row after row of graves, until finally, right in the middle of the back section, there it was—a nice granite marker with a small rusty anvil and ball peen hammer adjoined to the top.

But back to Wright Batchelor.

Terry brought in some old photos and a print that needed reframing for an upcoming fund-raiser. The group often raises money to replace Civil War veteran grave markers, in addition to participating in educational events. The members are as patriotic a group of Americans as you'll find. They are amateur historians, sleuths, and reenactors, certainly not a group to be associated with white supremacists. The photographic copies were a quick job, and when it came time to discuss charges, I offered him a deal.

"You told me once your wife had some information on some of my folks, right?"

"She most certainly does," he said. "She was a Batchelor."

"I'll tell you what, if she has anything on Wright Stephen Batchelor, bring me copies, and we can call it even."

"She has aplenty," Terry replied. "And that's a deal."

Then, he offered what he knew—quickly outlining things not included in the book entry I'd found, including specific war service, work at the county poor house, and a murder. Somewhere in the telling there was something about a "dog pissing on some tobacco," and it concluded with, "I can tell you where he's buried, but you don't want to go out there. That crazy fool woman that lives on that property will shoot you. Don't go." He claimed she had shot at him and a deputy one day.

"Surely, she won't shoot at someone trying to take a picture of a tombstone, if I stop and ask real nice."

He drew me a map of how to get there and admonished me again. Then he threw in this nugget: "You do know you're directly related to him [Batchelor], I assume?"

I did not know I was directly related to Wright. In forty years, I'd never once heard his name mentioned. The area where my mama grew up is thick with Batchelors, and I went to church with plenty current and former ones. My mother, now in her eighties, doesn't recall Wright ever being mentioned.

A genealogy search at Braswell Memorial Library Genealogy Room in Rocky Mount quickly resolved the mystery. The resources there are amazing for a city its size, and the materials are lovingly curated by librarians who value history. As it turned out, this man who was becoming more interesting by the minute was my great-great-grandfather. Mama's grandfather, who would have remembered his father, died when Mama was two years old. Around the time I was making these discoveries, I relocated a family tree that an old family friend known for the accuracy of her research had done years before, and it confirmed my information.

Terry came into the studio to pick up his work, and he had several sheets compiled by his wife, some that had been published in a local history newsletter, expanding only a little on Wright's war and postwar time, but two new items turned up: a photocopy of a photograph, probably taken just after the war, and the mention of a murder and subsequent trial in the 1880s.

A cousin had a copy of the photograph, and despite my assurances of never letting it leave the studio to be reproduced, she was reluctant to let me borrow it overnight but eventually let me come by to copy it at her house. A source in the Bryant notes mentioned a family Bible and an interview granted to Terry's wife by my great-uncle Needham (Needy) Batchelor. He told her a passed-down oral history of Wright's return from Appomattox, much of which was used to compose chapter 1 of this book.

I was at once excited and frustrated. The family friend who did the genealogy had passed away, and so had my great-uncle, making me about a decade too late in being able to get some insight. However, I figured some digging at the county courthouse and a search of old newspaper accounts would fill in my blanks. I had recently started my pursuit of another graduate degree, and my primary instructor for the semester had just published a book about the story of her family and how she had compiled the research after finding a chest of old letters. This whole thing would be easy enough, and I figured I'd get a twenty-page braided essay out of it, or if I was lucky, a chapter in what became my first book, *Memory Cards*. Little did I know an extensive chase was just beginning, with lots of frustration and satisfaction in between the hurdles and roadblocks.

Less than an hour east on Highway 64 from Raleigh, Nash County, couldn't be more different than the bustle of the state capital and the area known as the Triangle (Raleigh–Durham–Chapel Hill), an area with three major universities and numerous large companies. As far as differences in convenience, social scene, and "city life," it is more like a thousand miles. Raleigh and Wake County are booming in growth, opportunity, and economy, while Nash County has seen hard times since the 1990s, losing corporate headquarters, a once booming world tobacco market, and population in large numbers. It is very much still a rural place. I grew up in the same county as Wright Batchelor and have lived in it most of my life. In the 1980s one of my next-door neighbors traveled to town by mule and wagon, and there were numerous outhouses on my road, and at least one moonshiner.

The county, even in the twenty-first century, is still largely agricultural, much as it was in the mid-1860s. Instead of cotton and tobacco, sweet potatoes are king now—the county is the world's largest producer. There is also plenty of corn and soybeans, with some tobacco and cotton still around. Other than some roads being rerouted or meandering, and the fact there are a lot more people, it is not hard to imagine what the communities outside the county seat of Nashville (pop. 5,000) might have been like. Wright was from a crossroads just outside of town called White Oak. There is at least one other community in the southern end of the county that goes by the same name. Today White Oak has a church that predates the Civil War, a country store, and not much else besides fields and farms. There is a road named Old County Home Road that runs through it to another community named after a carpet-bagging sawmill operator from New York named Momeyer.[2] This is the approximate site of the original Nash County Poor House, on a site called Charity Plain according to records, but that was before it was broken up into pieces in the early twentieth century. Before and after the war, Wright was the superintendent on an on-and-off basis. The "crazy fool woman" Terry mentioned lives out that way, and I've yet to muster the courage to test her. Most of the present-day Batchelors are scattered in this area, more so toward Momeyer, where a number of them live and attend church. Most seem to have little or no knowledge or much more than a passing interest in the past of this man who seems so complicated, as is described in these pages—a reluctant rebel, an industrious farmer trying to improve his lot, and later a practitioner of contrary county politics and alliances not common to his social group.

Like any modern-day researcher and otherwise lazy writer might do, I started my search on the internet. There were only a hand-ful of newspapers in the county from that era, and precious few issues survived to be microfilmed or digitized. At Braswell Memo-rial Library in Rocky Mount I found family records and names of relatives and birth and death dates, as well as further confirmation of my relationship to Wright. I found conflicts in the research of others, some that even contradicted themselves on the same page. Many dates were wrong and events out of place, teaching me early on to always go back to original documents.

Having first found out from Terry's wife that Wright Stephen Batchelor was superintendent of the poor house after the war, I started looking for information about this government agency. A man had compiled minutes over a time period of just before the war to just after into a self-printed book titled *The Minutes of the War-dens of the Poor in Nash County*.[3] His last name is Rackley, which immediately caught my attention as a name related to the mur-der case about which I had scant information. I was sure it was no coincidence. The minutes gave a time frame but also proved contradictory when I tried to lay out a timeline of Wright's service. He and several members of his family and his wife's family not only had served in various roles but also supplied items and services to the poor house. Some years were missing.

There was very little in the way of wartime information either on the county or in newspaper searches. A return trip to Broadfoot Publishing Company landed me a copy of *North Carolina Troops*, the regimental histories of North Carolina's units. There I found a beautifully written summary of Company A of the Forty-Seventh North Carolina Regiment by its captain, John Hall Thorp (sometimes spelled as Thorpe) of Rocky Mount. It gave much information on locations and movements and general engagements but was compiled by Thorp almost forty years after the events happened, when there was a fever pitch across the South and the state to memorialize and honor Confederate dead, as those veterans who survived were beginning to die out in large numbers. Thorp, backed by a prominent local Confederate veteran, Col. R. H. Ricks, compiled and published a list of those who served. Ricks was also instrumental in the construction of a Confederate monument, which was later moved from its original location to the entrance of Battle Park in Rocky Mount on private property.

Thorp must have kept contact with Batchelor after the war, even though the men lived about twenty miles apart. Thorp served on the poor house board during the time Batchelor was in charge.

Newspaper reports, when they could be found, proved to offer little, other than a Missing in Action blurb on Batchelor after battles at Gettysburg and Bristoe Station. Wright left little behind in the form of written records, other than apparently updating the family Bible, which belongs to the folks who inherited the estate of my Uncle Needy. At least one census prior to the war listed Wright as unable to read or write, and all those after the war list him as literate; his standing in the postwar community would imply that he almost had to have some education to serve in his role as superintendent, which he also did before the war. Census taking was at best a slipshod endeavor at the time, and inaccuracies are many.

Perhaps my biggest indicator of how hard it would be piecing together the puzzle of an ordinary man from the time period was when I began the search for trial records of the strange murder case after the war involving this man. Newspaper accounts varied wildly, some even confusing the victim and the assailant, proving fake news has a longer history than most realize. Multiple jails, counties, and sheriffs were listed as locations of the prisoner and the trial. Finally, I went to the courthouse to try to find original documents, or some digital version of such. Although state funds had been made available, not all of the records had been digitized.

I stuck my head in three doors in the old 1921 courthouse hallway. Each clerk politely informed me I wasn't in the right place and referred me elsewhere. Eventually I landed at the right counter, in criminal records, which was manned by a friend from church.

"Hey Jessica, I need some help finding an arrest record," I said.

"Okay, sure. Do you have the dates or names?"

"Yes." I gave her some names and then offered: "And the date is November 6, 1886."

Jessica's shoulders dropped, and she stopped typing on the computer and looked up at me, and I noticed folks at some surrounding desks had taken note.

"You're kidding, right?" she asked.

"Of course not. Can you pull that up?"

"Uh, no. That's probably in the basement. Maybe. Somewhere."

I'd already been warned about the basement from a previous inquiry in another office. Jessica sent me back there. Another friend happened to work in that office, and after a brief discussion on the dangers of the basement, which included dampness, darkness, mold, mildew, and potentially deadly, wild animals, I was assured someone would check it out and call me. My hopes were not high. About a week later, the call came.

"Mike, there aren't any records to be found from 1886," my friend said. "There's been fires and flooding down there since then, and those things probably got destroyed."

I was not completely surprised, given the age of the documents, but I certainly felt my dream of finding enough information to create a long essay slipping away. These were the stories that had become interesting to me, the stories about real people, regular people. There are a million biographies out there on the famous, the leaders, Robert E. Lee, Stonewall Jackson, Jefferson Davis, Abraham Lincoln, U. S. Grant, et al. But there were very few about the people who served in the ranks, what their time was like, and what happened to them after the war.

By that point, I'd also run into a wall at the library with my search of newspapers. Other than knowing that Wright fathered more children, that he ran the poor house for a time, and that there was an investigation, my leads had run out. My class assignment would remain open-ended, literally with no ending; my professor sympathized that this happens, and sometimes you can fill in the blanks, sometimes you can't, and sometimes you just make your story fiction based on truth. I wasn't quite ready to quit, though, at least until I gave a little more chase. I could only think of one more long shot, and I would have to postpone that until I had more time. I needed to make a trip to Raleigh, to the state archives.

3

The Rip Van Winkle State

O! that our State, . . . would wake up from her Rip Van Winkle
agricultural sleep! and, for her own best interests, would become
a reader and extensive patronizer of the *North Carolina
Farmer* and other agricultural periodicals!

—Letter writer to the *North Carolina Farmer,* 1845

During the first half of the nineteenth century, North Carolina
seemed unaware of much that was going on anywhere,
even within its own boundaries.

—WILLIAM S. POWELL, Tar Heel historian

Sixty years passed from the time Giovanni da Verranzo first spotted natives at the mouth of the Cape Fear River until Sir Walter Raleigh's ill-fated group of colonists landed on Roanoke Island in 1584. Almost another century would pass before the Carolina Charter in 1663 granted the Lords Proprietors a new colony.

North Carolina was still a wild place when the Lords Proprietors sold their shares and North Carolina became mostly a royal colony. Topographically it divides neatly into three parts: the coastal plain (east), the piedmont (central), and the mountains (west). For forty years there was no firmly established capital—it was wherever the governor happened to live. There were no "cities" to speak of, so the commercial centers of the eastern part of the state rotated the hosting of the Assembly: Edenton, Wilmington, and New Bern.

Royal Governor Arthur Dobbs tried to establish a permanent capital near present-day Kinston on the Neuse River, which was to be called George City. His successor, William Tryon, managed to get a permanent palace built in New Bern. Taxes used to build the extravagant structure, along with other charges of corruption, helped bring on the Regulator Rebellion from 1768 to 1771, an event many historians consider a key step toward the American Revolution.

Later, in April 1776, a resolution was adopted by the Fourth Provincial Congress of North Carolina, which met in the town of Halifax. This document encouraged all the delegates to the Continental Congress to push for independence and later became known as the Halifax Resolves, key in the provenance of the Declaration of Independence three months later.

There was not much action in North Carolina during the Revolution, and there were no cities of substantial size after the war. The state was mostly wilderness. From 1777 to 1791 the legislature moved through seven different towns. Tarboro, Fayetteville, and Hillsborough all had designs on becoming the permanent capital. In the end a place was chosen that wasn't actually even a city. In 1787 an ordinance was proposed that would establish the capital in Wake County, within ten miles of Isaac Hunter's tavern. It took four years to pass, and in 1792 the state purchased a thousand acres from Joel Lane. The city of Raleigh was born around the fledgling center of government.

Life in North Carolina was so unchanged from the Revolutionary War period that it earned the nickname "the Rip van Winkle State." Nash County was formed out of Edgecombe County—a significant center of wealth and influence in the antebellum era—in 1777. The new county was named for Gen. Francis Nash, one of George Washington's favorite commanders, who died at the Battle of Germantown (Pennsylvania) on October 4, 1777. Just over a month later, prominent planter Nathan Boddie introduced a bill in the legislature to slice off part of Edgecombe at what was then called the Falls of the Tar River.[1] Because of the size of the county, it was difficult for the citizenry to attend court, public meetings, and vote. Parts of several other counties would later be formed out of Edgecombe, such as Granville (1746), Halifax (1758), and Wilson (1855, with parts of Nash, Johnston, and Wayne as well). Among the 254 locals who signed a petition in support of the bill were Wright's kinfolk, William, Stephen, and Samuel Batchelor. (Note: Also on the list was one of the patriarchs of the other side of my family, Jacob Brantley, proving the long-held suspicion that my family was not only poor as dirt but old as it as well.)[2] Three acres were purchased from one of the area's largest landowners, Micajah Thomas, for ten pounds on April 4, 1780.[3]

A temporary courthouse was built in the town then called Nash Courthouse in 1778, and a permanent one was erected in 1784 on what was then called Peachtree Street but is now known as Washington Street. That courthouse was replaced with one in 1834 that lasted until the early twentieth century. There were no major Revolutionary War battles fought in the county, although Gen. Charles Cornwallis camped near Rocky Mount on his way toward destiny at Yorktown in 1781.

Nash Courthouse became Nashville in 1815. In 1820 there were 8,185 citizens of Nash County, and by 1860 the population had only grown by 3,500 residents. Nash County was a sleepy enclave in a sleepy state in the 1820s when Wright was born. The state was overwhelmingly rural, and most of the inhabitants were farmers who had managed to purchase their own farms, however small they might be. The *Fayetteville Observer* reported in 1837, "The great mass of our population is composed of people who cultivate their own soil, owe no debt, and live within their means. It is true we have no overgrown fortunes, but it is also true that we have few beggars."[4]

Agriculture drove the lives of the people, and everything revolved around it. It informed every decision. Forget what the movies show about the Old South: a slow-moving, laid-back life of gentleman planters sipping mint juleps on the veranda while the ladies sat around in hoop skirts, sipping tea and rolling off honey-dripped drawling accents about the upcoming cotillions. That was not the case in North Carolina. The majority of citizens were yeoman farmers, and there were a large number of free blacks. Some were landowners, some were tenant farmers, and some were paid servants.

While there were three thousand plantations of one thousand acres or more, there were also forty-six thousand farms of one hundred acres or fewer.[5] North Carolina never developed an extensive plantation system like Virginia and South Carolina.

By 1850 Nashville was still small but boasted a tailor, a bookmaker, a surveyor, a general store, a carriage shop, and a male academy. In the 1840 census, 3,133 men are listed as farmers, while only 66 are categorized as working in manufacturing. The Falls at Rocky Mount was a mill village that developed when Joseph Battle formed Rocky Mount Mills in 1818. This was this beginning of a textile industry that would flourish in North Carolina for 180 years. But when the railroad came through in 1840, a town grew up around the depot, about a mile away. Rocky Mount became the county's largest city and eventually straddled the Nash-Edgecombe county line. Nash was often disparaged as the "uncouth offspring of Edgecombe . . . [an] area of whiskey and taverns." There were, in fact, at least twenty taverns on record in the county between 1836 and 1860. After agriculture, turpentine production was the second largest industry in Nash County.[6]

North Carolina's staple crops were wheat, corn, and rice, and there were two main cash crops—tobacco and cotton. Cotton production nearly doubled from 1850 to 1860, with 145,000 bales being produced just before hostilities broke out. In 1850, 12 million pounds of tobacco came out of the fields, and by 1860 that figure had nearly tripled to 33 million.[7] In the South, North Carolina was second to last in cotton; second in sweet potatoes, peas, and oats; third in rice, tobacco, wheat, and Irish potatoes. The number of farms grew to sixty-seven thousand, and 69 percent of them were less than a hundred acres. One-third of the population was enslaved, and twelve counties had more slaves than free whites. The state was seventh in slaves and fifth in slave owners. North Carolina was second only to Virginia in the number of free people of color.[8]

In the antebellum South some ministers promoted slavery as a positive practice, "ordained by God to Christianize heathen Africans and uplift the white folks who owned them."[9] Religion was a key part of life in North Carolina, and Baptists (most members) and Methodists (most churches) were the dominant denominations. Quakers were the foremost opponents to slavery. Slavery "contributed to the agricultural enslavement of that section of the country," and it was "impossible for white or free black labor to compete. Artisans and skilled European immigrants stayed in the North, and left the South without a lot of intelligent and skilled" workers.[10]

Instead of big cities, North Carolina was mostly small towns and communities. Two railroads served the state, the Wilmington to Weldon in the east and the North Carolina Railroad in the western piedmont. No town boasted a population over 10,000, and only two exceeded 5,000: Wilmington (9,552) and New Bern (5,432). The other largest cities in the antebellum period were Fayetteville (4,790) and Raleigh (4,780).[11] The commercial centers were often crossroads country stores or grist mills, and much of the social life was centered around church—about half the population were members of one denomination or another. While there was the University of North Carolina in Chapel Hill, most of the citizens did not have much, if any, formal education, and relatively few could read or write. Even though the legislature passed an education bill in 1839 to set up a statewide school system, not much was done until the years just before the Civil War, and even then participation was spotty. Not every county had schools, and those that did only allowed whites to attend.

This was the life Wright came into when his mother, Hulda Vaughn Batchelor, the second wife of patriarch Daniel Batchelor, gave birth on May 25, 1828. Wright was his mother's fourth child in five years, and Daniel's eighth child. Daniel fathered twelve offspring by three wives before he passed at age eighty—his last wife giving birth to twins when he was seventy-five.

Wright had three older half brothers by Daniel's first wife, Ann Tucker Batchelor: Bennett, born in 1789; Drewery, born in 1790; and Daniel Jr., born in 1795. There was also an older half sister, Pheraby, born in 1819.

He had two full sisters, Elizabeth (1823) and Mahalia (1827), as well as brothers Vincent (1825) and Ruffin (1831), the latter of whom he was closest to. In 1832 Daniel married a third wife, Nancy

Creekmore, who gave birth to Francis that year and twin girls, Louisa and Emeliza, in 1848.

The Batchelors, like most farmers of the time, produced almost all of what they needed right there on the farm and disposed of any excess to purchase the other things they needed. They grew row crops and raised pigs. Other than more homes, in some ways the area known as White Oak hasn't changed much, with one store, which sells convenience items and does auto repairs, and one church, which still meets, albeit on an irregular basis.

The men spent long days in the fields and around the barns, plowing, planting, hoeing, and weeding the crops, as well as feeding and caring for the animals. The children had chores such as milking and shoveling out stalls or hauling water, depending on age and gender, and the women cooked and cleaned and kept house, sometimes helping in the fields when it was demanded. Providing food and keeping shelter in good order drove everyday life, and cash was a secondary consideration. Day laborers earned twenty-five to fifty cents a day, and usually room and board. Feeding the livestock, milking, and picking up eggs were jobs for the children. When landowners passed away, the older son usually got the land, the youngest son got the main house, and the daughters got home furnishings and cash. Entertainment was limited to time on the front porch, or at neighbors' homes, involving conversation or sometimes music, often stringed instruments such as guitars, fiddles, and banjos, the roots of old time and bluegrass beginning to take hold. Sundays when church was in session—many area congregations shared ministers who rotated assignments each week—provided time not only for worship but also for visiting, gossiping, swapping news and stories, and, of course, scouting out prospects of the opposite sex for marriage. Church was a big deal. There was a strong sense of community.

In his early twenties Wright was already working on becoming his own man, having been hired as overseer of local widow Martha Battle's farm. Even though he couldn't read or write (according to the census), Wright was given great responsibility on the Battle farm, which was divided between Martha and her sons. The 1860 census shows the widow as the owner of eighty slaves, making her one of the wealthiest persons around. Her plantation was worth $5,000 at the time (nearly $150,000 in today's money), and her sons Lucian, twenty-one, and twins Alexander and William, nineteen, each had $550 stakes. Oddly, the census listed the twins as students, and all three boys as married and able to both read and write. Wright's management skills would pay dividends in the coming years and allow him to advance socially.

President Millard Fillmore's Compromise of 1850 that ended the slave trade in Washington DC also made the punishment for fugitive slaves more severe. While this outraged the growing number of abolitionists in the country, it did little to satiate the wealthy slave owners of some of the other Southern states. California was added as a free state. South Carolina, Georgia, and Mississippi were already secretly considering ways to leave the Union. The overwhelming majority of North Carolinians, while they may have passively supported slavery, had no desire to break off from the United States, mostly because of security concerns and a large, irregular coastline that provided ample vulnerabilities from potential invaders.

The state's constitution had a complete makeover by the legislature in 1835 and was tweaked repeatedly throughout the nineteenth century. Only white men who owned fifty acres could vote for state senators, and the House was based on population. Election of the governor was given over to the voters. The ban on Catholics holding public office was lifted, but not that on Jews or atheists (these restrictions were not limited to North Carolina or the South). Free blacks and Indians were prevented from voting, largely based on the fallout and fear of rebellion after Nat Turner's uprising in 1831. Slave uprisings were a clear and present danger in the minds of both slaveholders and non-slaveholders across the South, and North Carolina was no exception. Turner's Virginia killing spree left fifty-seven dead, including women and children, and terrified whites for decades. This no doubt supports the theory of how so many who did not own slaves may have convinced themselves that the evil institution was necessary. Free blacks and slaves were restricted from preaching, carrying arms, and discussing politics, and lim-

its were placed on travel and how they were able to defend themselves in court.[12] "Free" was a relative term.

The state legislature held elections in 1839, and sixty-one of
sixty-eight counties voted for schools. Nash County got nine districts, with Josiah Vick placed as chairman of the superintendents.
There were thirty-one schools for whites, and the average school
term was three months. It was illegal to teach slaves to read and
write. By the time the war was underway, only eight of thirty-one
schools remained open.

Wright continued to work and found his mate, Sally Ann Ward.
They married on June 18, 1851, on the farm of her parents, Willis Ward and Lucy Tucker Ward, just down the road. Thirty people attended the service presided over by a justice of the peace, the
honorable John H. Drake Jr., who was also the local doctor. The
couple had their own piece of land and started their life together.
By 1860 Wright and Sally Ann had $350 worth of real estate and
$275 worth of personal property. They had 200 acres of improved
land and another 100 acres of unimproved land. The farm was valued at $2,100 and included 4 horses, 6 milk cows, 3 oxen, 6 cattle,
100 pigs, 1,000 bushels of Indian corn, 80 bushels of oats, 6 400-
pound bales of cotton, 140 bushels of beans and peas, 20 bushels of
Irish potatoes, 500 bushels of sweet potatoes, $50 worth of orchard
products, 5 pounds of beeswax, and $360 worth of slaughtered ani-
mals. The census also listed Wright as a turpentine laborer, among
his other duties, but there is no other record of his working in this
area to be found. Ruffin is listed in the same census as a turpentine
worker as well, and it could be the brothers were in business together
or working for a local producer in addition to farming. Ruffin married Sallie Ann Batchelor—that's no misprint; brothers Wright and
Ruffin both married women named Sally (Sallie) Ann. Ruffin and
his Sallie had four children: Sarah Jane, born on Christmas Day in
1854, Richard in 1858, Cornelia in 1859, and Mourning in 1862.

Sally Ann Ward Batchelor's mother and Wright's mother-in-law,
Lucy, widowed in 1859, was living with the Batchelors by 1860, but
she was no burden. She owned $675 worth of real estate and had
personal property of another $170. The children all worked on the

farm, and Eugenia was the only one who had "attempted school within the year." Wright had also taken a couple of turns running the Nash County Poor House and was superintendent in 1860, having served in that role in 1853 and from 1856 to 1858. While Wright and Sally Ann were not wealthy by any stretch, things were looking up for them as the clouds of war darkened and threatened even this small backcountry farm.

North Carolina's makeup was not like that of many other states. By 1860 only 28 percent of the population owned slaves, and 70 percent of them had fewer than 10 slaves.[13] Nash County had a population of 11,867 and had more free blacks (687) than slaves (468). In neighboring Edgecombe there were 17,376 residents and 10,108 slaves, and right next door to the west, Franklin County was listed at 14,107 citizens and 7,076 slaves.[14] Most of the farms were small, and each owner and his family did the majority of the labor or used hired hands.

Six distinct social classes can be sorted out. At the top was the gentry, or the planter class. This was about 6 percent of the white population and was made up of plantation owners, public officials, lawyers, doctors and businessmen. This was the smallest class, but it controlled the state government, where power was largely based on land ownership and wealth.

Next was the middle class, which was about 25 percent of the white population and was composed of most of the rest of the slaveowners. Manufacturers, lower-ranking public officials, professionals of modest income, and small farmers formed this class, and most aspired to step up to the level of the gentry.

Wright fell into the third class, known as common whites. This was where most North Carolinians fell, somewhere between 60 and 65 percent of the population. These folks owned land but not slaves. They raised crops and livestock for personal use, and if there was any surplus it was used to pay off debt or trade for needed items. It was difficult to advance from this group of yeoman farmers, artisans, tradesmen, miners, mechanics, overseers, and naval store workers.

After common whites came poor whites. These landless, mostly illiterate citizens made up 5 to 10 percent of the population and held the lowest-level jobs. Although they did not own slaves, they supported the institution, were often vocal about it, and served in militias and slave patrols. When the war came, most of the troops were drawn from this pool, lending credence to the phrase "a rich man's war, but a poor man's fight."

North Carolina had a large number of free blacks, and figures from 1860 numbered them at 30,463, with two-thirds being considered mulatto, or mixed race. Wilmington, New Bern, and Halifax had large numbers of free blacks, and many owned farms, ran small businesses, and in some cases even owned slaves. Many common whites and poor whites saw free blacks as their primary competition.

At the bottom of the social chain, obviously, was the slave population. Slaves were in every county and made up one-third of the state's labor force, although the highest concentration was in the eastern part of the state where the largest plantations existed.[15]

In 1861 the working population in the United States was 7.7 million, of which 4.9 million were farmers. There was no collective ID, lives were all different, and government was a much more abstract idea.[16]

It would be the planter class, combined with geography and the early, fraught decisions of Lincoln that would force a war on all of these classes; it was a war that few favored and for which many would foot the bill in treasure and life.

4

A New Life in the Face of an Approaching National Storm

There never was a time when, in my opinion, some way could
not be found to prevent the drawing of the sword.

—Gen. Ulysses S. Grant

Wright and Sally Ann started their life together just when the United
States was coming apart. There was a gathering storm in the country, winds of war that were already starting to blow.

In April 1853 Sally Ann gave birth to the Batchelors' first child,
Eugenia, and another baby, Lucy Jane, followed the next September. By May 1856 the family had grown to five with the birth of
William, and the White Oak household was a beehive, with three
children under the age of four. Large families were commonplace,
and the young couple was well on its way.

In 1853 Wright, twenty-five, was named superintendent of the
Nash County Poor House. This would be evidence that the young
farmer was not just succeeding in the fields but was gaining respect
and a reputation for honesty and management. Both he and Sally
Ann had been paid for work done for the poor house over the years.
It also appears that Wright had given up his job with the Widow
Battle as overseer of her plantation operations. This offers the first
sign that Wright may have been struggling with his conscience and
thoughts on slavery. He never owned slaves, there is no record of
him mistreating them, and there is no evidence or suggestion that
he ever aspired to own other men, as his later actions supported.

It could be that like many North Carolinians, his only support for slavery was his lack of vocal or direct action to abolish it.

In the early days of the colony there wasn't tremendous disparity in wealth, as survival depended on food production for currency. As times changed and some began to prosper more than others as the colony grew, the church was primarily responsible for helping those in need. In 1755 a law was passed by the General Assembly for "relief of the poor and the prevention of idleness." Later, in 1817, a tax was approved, and through private donations and will bequests, funding for the poor slowly came about. Not much was done formally until well into the antebellum period, when the Nash County Wardens of the Poor was formed, and in 1834 the organization purchased 238 acres from local planter Henry Blount to build the area's first poor house. The deed refers to the property as lying along Little "Sappone" Creek (spelled Sapony now). The area was referred to as Charity Plain. The wardens included some of the best-known citizens at that time and surnames that endure to this day in Nash County: Turner Westray, John Ricks, James Dozier, James Harrison, Thomas Savage, Marmaduke Ricks, and Hardy Pridgen. The price tag was $317.33.[1]

The new poor house and its necessary buildings would be funded by property taxes and managed by a rotating board of wardens. A superintendent or overseer was appointed and contracted each year, and citizens nominated for the board faced penalties for refusing to serve. The wardens had great latitude in how funds were used, and records from the time show payments for food, clothing, and whiskey (for medicinal purposes), as well as reimbursing citizens for caring for or transporting residents to the poor house, sewing, and services such as coffin building and ditch digging.

There were four methods of caring for the poor in North Carolina:

1. An allowance could be given to the pauper.

2. The pauper could be "let" on contract to a farmer, manufacturer, or businessperson.

3. The pauper could be sold or a contract made with an individual to take care of the pauper.

4. The pauper could be admitted to the poor house.

Not just anyone could show up and check into a room, however. Strict rules were in place to avoid abuse and fraud. Persons had to be incapable of making a living, either physically or mentally, or had to be "afflicted, idiots, insane, invalids, cripples or old." Children were to be apprenticed if possible. The Nash County Poor House was a working farm and as self-sufficient as possible, which was as popular a concept at the time as prison farms and shops are now. There was a superintendent's house, a smoke house, smaller houses or dorms for the residents, tobacco barns, and other small outbuildings. Life was no picnic, and a letter to the *Tarborough Press* in neighboring Edgecombe County summed it up best, stating the purpose of the poor house should be "to graduate the support of paupers to the very lowest point fit for mankind, otherwise they would offer inducements to pauperism."[2] Even so, poor houses usually provided comfortable space, and most were constructed to have small rooms with a fireplace that connected to a large common room for meals and church. Although residents were considered unable to live independently, they were expected to tend to the livestock and work in the fields.

Wright handled the purchasing and budgeting and made sure crops were planted, tended, harvested, and stored. He had to assign rooms, manage work assignments and disputes among the "inmates," as the residents were often called, and report to the board that he was running a tight and efficient ship, while providing service to those in the community who could not take care of themselves.

In 1854 the position of warden became a paid position, and the title was changed to superintendent. The next two years Wright's brother Daniel Jr. was put in charge of the poor house, and records show the brothers' father lived on the grounds. Reports show him as a pauper, but it is more likely that he lived with Daniel in the superintendent's house. Daniel Sr. would have been about eighty at the time. Wright then took the job each year from 1856 to 1859, and in 1860 A. F. Lewis took over as what the minutes termed "overseer."

Inflamed Passions

The formation of the Republican Party in 1856, with its aggressive antislavery stance, inflamed many of the Southern states and caused concern in North Carolina. As regional and national politics arced toward a fiery, fever pitch in the mid-1850s, and the fire-breathers and hawks started clamoring for secession and use of force, North Carolinians wanted no part of the nonsense. While very few owned slaves, most citizens supported it—it was the one issue that secessionists and conservatives alike shared.

The talk of secession wasn't a new idea to the country. In the early days of the country the New England States threatened to secede if the Assumption Bill didn't pass—a bill that would allow the federal government to assume the debts occurred during the War of Independence by the states. The southern states had been more successful in paying off their debts and opposed the bill. Compromise allowed the bill to pass, with the establishment of Washington in the "South." In 1798 North Carolina judge John K. Taylor had suggested secession as a possible response to "undesirable" federal legislation, at a time when the country and Constitution were in their infancy.[3] Some New England Federalists promoted the idea of secession in 1801 when Thomas Jefferson was elected president and again over the Louisiana Purchase. The issue came up again in New England during the War of 1812, when the northern states felt their shipping interests were not being considered (there was even a convention called in Hartford, Connecticut).[4] At another time, both Vermont and Kentucky considered withdrawing from the Union, and ever-troublesome South Carolina first took up the issue in 1828 and again in 1832 because of tariffs.[5] Congress authorized Andrew Jackson to use force if necessary to get the state to comply, which proved not to be necessary. Other rattlings came up over the Missouri Compromise and the Dred Scott decision, and a convention was held in Nashville in 1850 to discuss "Northern aggression" and present a united front from the Southern states.

However, in the years leading up to the Civil War, North Carolina's constitution did not permit secession, and its voters did not wish it. State senator Jones B. Shepherd of Wake County said in 1850 that the state could secede from the Union just as easily as it joined, but most of his fellow citizens and legislators disagreed, and his efforts to move the idea were overwhelmingly defeated.[6]

Governor Thomas Bragg, from Nash's neighboring county, Warren, was elected in 1854 and served two, two-year terms. Although
Bragg, the older brother of the soon-to-be Confederate general
Braxton Bragg, was an ardent states-rights Democrat, he was more
interested in expanding the number of citizens with voting privi-
leges, improving the banking system, and developing more infrastructure in the state such as roads, railroads, canals, harbors, and
bridges than fomenting secession. The state had been slow to agree
to fund such improvement projects and had paid for it with lack
of economic growth.[7]

Bragg urged moderation in resisting federal reach, and although
his public comments against secession were limited, he considered it a disastrous choice. After his appointment to the Senate in
1859, he reluctantly resigned a few months before secession and
was expelled when he joined the Confederacy as attorney general
in 1861.

His successor as governor was fellow Democrat and judge John
Willis Ellis, another states-rights advocate, slaveholder, and aris-
tocrat who would quickly turn from moderate to hawkish in his
support for leaving the Union. At the time Ellis was elected, he
said, "Grievous as are these causes of discontent, we are not prepared for the acknowledgement that we cannot enjoy all our constitutional rights in the Union."[8] Of course, in his view, foremost
among those constitutional rights was slavery. Ellis defeated William Woods Holden, a leading Democrat who had helped many
successful politicians gain office but who was considered "unpol-
ished" by many of his contemporaries, in part because he was an
illegitimate child (even though he was accepted into the Holden
family). Holden was a good politician and came to the public eye
when he became editor of the *North Carolina Standard* in 1843, at
age twenty-five. He made it the leading paper in the state and built
his name by standing up for common people. Although defeated,
Holden would become a vocal force against his former political
allies during the war.

That same year, in September, Sally Ann Batchelor gave birth
to a daughter named Kansas, Arkansas, or Cancis, depending on

the source. No one knows why the child got this moniker, since both Wright and Sally Ann did not have much formal education, had no known relatives in either Arkansas or the Territory of Kansas, had not traveled out of state, and apparently could not read or write. This is where one has to again wonder about the politics of Wright. Despite the lack of formal education, the interactions of his job and his place in the community indicate he would have closely followed and kept up with the news and politics of the day. The Kansas-Nebraska Act of 1854 created the territories of Kansas and Nebraska and was intended by those in Washington to expand the Union and further push along the idea of a transcontinental railroad. Because of the timing, a pre–Civil War conflict occurred in "Bleeding Kansas," as pro-slavery and abolitionist forces descended on the region, first armed with words and later with rifles, to battle over the moral soul of the future state. Once again, the deviling of the Missouri Compromise came into play and was for all practical purposes irrelevant with the Act. Kansas entered the Union as a free state in January 1861. Was the naming of this child another hint of where the Batchelors stood? What was the talk in the stores and out on the streets of Nashville, where certainly the issues facing the country, while far removed from the remote areas of eastern North Carolina, were discussed and debated? Slavery, aside from its inherent wrongness, served no purpose to yeoman farmers such as Wright and most of his neighbors. If anything, it made free labor harder to come by. In Raleigh among those in power, slavery was far more important, as evidenced by a resolution issued by the Council of State in 1860 that read in part, "If we cannot hold our slave property, and at the same time enjoy repose and tranquility in the Union, we will be constrained, in justice to ourselves and our prosperity, to establish new forms."[9]

Hinton Rowan Helper of Davie County published a book in 1857 called *The Impending Crisis of the South: How to Meet It*, which caused a stir. The book called for freeing the slaves, and it was lauded by abolitionists and banned in the South. Helper said that a small group of rich aristocrats was oppressing whites with the institution of slavery. Helper, who had left North Carolina, was not welcome back in his home state. As further evidence of the complex and often tangled thinking of the people at the time, though, Helper was no advocate for rights for blacks—he felt slavery suppressed the demand for white workers. Helper used statistics to show how slavery was holding back the South, but he wanted blacks sent to colonies in Africa after they were freed. After the war he was seen as a white supremacist, and it was said that he even stopped eating at restaurants that employed blacks.

Ellis won reelection in 1860, but the margin was more narrow than the previous election. The governor sent mixed signals, while the populace made it clear over and over that it had no desire to leave the Union. In national elections, North Carolina voted for pro-Union Democrats, as Vice President John Breckenridge carried the day, with Abraham Lincoln left off the ballot entirely. Many Southerners hoped that a peace would be reached and that the federal government would reimburse slaveowners when the slaves were freed. Abolitionists wanted slavery ended without compensation.

Another daughter, Bunnion, was born to Wright and Sally Ann in September that year, not far from her sister (Ar)Kansas's birthday. Ellis addressed the legislature in November, not calling for secession but for "prevention . . . of civil war and preservation of peace." At the same time, he urged that North Carolina send representatives to meet with other states on the subject of secession. By the Southern Convention in January, he was urging delegates to get on with the business of forming the Confederacy and referred to North Carolina and Virginia as "border slave states." Ellis urged members of the Southern Convention meeting in Montgomery, Alabama, not to wait for the Virginia delegates to arrive as "Virginia, North Carolina and other border slave states will much sooner join an organized government than secede without such government."[10]

Some firebrands tried to jump the gun a month earlier in December 1860 and seized Fort Caswell and Fort Johnston in Wilmington. Governor Ellis ordered them to evacuate and informed President James Buchanan. Secessionists held meetings in Cleveland County in the west and New Hanover County in the east. The entire state was in upheaval, convulsion, and chaos.

Voters like Wright rejected this notion, as most had adopted a wary "watch and wait" attitude toward the election of Abraham Lincoln. Ellis himself even stated that the election of Lincoln alone did not pose a threat to North Carolina. Democrat John Breckenridge and Constitutional Unionist John Bell were on the ballot (Stephen Douglas was not) and supported the Union, although Breckenridge favored the right of secession. Most were angry with their neighbors in South Carolina who had left the Union in the previous December, escalating national tensions. To North Carolinians, the North seemed far away in distance and in philosophy. Numerous pro-Union forces placed the blame for the trouble squarely on South Carolina, while pro-secessionists such as Ellis and others blamed Republicans and national attempts to end slavery and escalated the fears of many whites that more slave uprisings might be on the horizon if North Carolina didn't withdraw from the Union.

Despite all this, voters narrowly rejected a convention on secession at the end of February by a vote of 47,338–46,672. Nash County support was lopsided at 989–93 votes "for" a convention, and the Edgecombe-Wilson vote was even more so at 1,588–17.[11] Most voters supported slavery but not secession and certainly not military action, and the state's internal opposition to secession was the sharpest of all Southern states. A group of men from Nash and Edgecombe counties went to Washington in early 1861 to meet with Lincoln and discuss ways to maintain peace, some pressing the narrative that reparations for slaveowners would have made for a "gradual and orderly event."[12] Ironically, Unionists would have held 80 of the 120 seats had a vote taken place. Many voters no doubt voted "for" a convention for this reason. In his March 4, 1861, inaugural address Lincoln assured citizens there would be no invasion of the South, and no interference where slavery already existed. The state legislature, dominated by the gentry, went around that sentiment after Ellis called them to session in May. North Carolina congressman Zebulon B. Vance, who had been outspoken in questioning the wisdom—but not legality—of secession urged restraint and said, "We have everything to gain and nothing to lose by delay, but too hasty action we make may take a fatal step we can never retrace . . . [we] may lose a heritage we can never recover."[13]

In the meantime, on April 12, 1861, Fort Sumter in Charleston Harbor was fired on by South Carolina troops and surrendered the next day. The state's and the country's fates were sealed when Lincoln called for seventy-five thousand troops to "coerce" the seceded states, and specifically for two regiments from North Carolina. Ellis's infamous reply was, "You shall get no troops from North Carolina." This was too much for even staunch Union men: North Carolina would not send troops to "invade" or fire on its neighbors. Kentucky governor Beriah Magoffin, whose state did not leave the Union, was even more sharp in his words, refusing to send troops "for the wicked purpose of subduing her sister southern states."[14] All of the North Carolina newspapers that had supported the Union changed course. The states were suddenly bound by one common fear that hadn't existed previously: invasion from the North. Ellis ordered the Wilmington forts to be seized, as well as Fort Macon, farther north up the coast near Morehead City. The federal arsenal in Fayetteville was seized, as was all federal property in the state, and troops were offered to Virginia. The legislature repealed a statute that state officers had to continue their oath to support the U.S. Constitution, and it authorized ten regiments and called for fifty thousand volunteers to serve for the duration of hostilities, plus twelve months. North Carolina had five cannon at the time.

Nash County sent one of its top five wealthiest planters, Archibald Hunter Arrington (who was worth over $100,000) of the Hilliardston community to Raleigh, and the debate was on. Arrington, who had chaired the secession convention held in Nashville, was conflicted, as evidenced by his personal notes and papers. As he prepared to represent Wright and the other people of county, he laid out "Two Questions," the territorial question and the question of slavery, noting the 1820 Missouri Compromise and the Dred Scott decision. He wrote that all states had slavery in 1777, and that when Massachusetts outlawed it in 1787, they gave themselves twenty years to phase out the practice, implying that such rational moves were now not on the table. Arrington noted the moral conflict as well, writing that it is "sinful to hold slaves—there are two modes to abolish it—constitutional by circumvention—forcible by hostile laws and insurrections."[15] Perhaps nothing better shows the conflicted mindset of the people of the time than the fact that a church-going slaveowner would note that his own actions were "sinful."

Arrington was outraged at Lincoln's call for troops in particular and wouldn't even call the president by name in his writings and remarks: "For the first time in the history of our government we have a President elected to rule over us who dares not go into 15 states of the Union and avow his prize—he would be indicted and punished as a seditious mercenary—he dare not put his foot in No. Carolina."[16]

Fearing the reality that voters would reject secession, the legislature unilaterally passed an ordinance of secession:

> AN ORDINANCE to dissolve the union between the State of North Carolina and the other States united with her, under the compact of government entitled "The Constitution of the United States."
>
> We, the people of the State of North Carolina in convention assembled, do declare and ordain, and it is hereby declared and ordained, That the ordinance adopted by the State of North Carolina in the convention of 1789, whereby the Constitution of the United States was ratified and adopted, and also all acts and parts of acts of the General Assembly ratifying and adopting amendments to the said Constitution, are hereby repealed, rescinded, and abrogated.
>
> We do further declare and ordain, That the union now subsisting between the State of North Carolina and the other States, under the title of the United States of America, is hereby dissolved, and that the State of North Carolina is in full possession and exercise of all those rights of sovereignty which belong and appertain to a free and independent State.
>
> Done in convention at the city of Raleigh, this the 20th day of May, in the year of our Lord 1861, and in the eighty-fifth year of the independence of said State.[17]

An amendment was hastily proposed to put the ordinance to popular vote, but it was defeated 72–34, as rejection was virtually guaranteed. Virginia and Tennessee had allowed the people to have the final say, but North Carolinians would not get the chance. Realistically, though, being surrounded by Confederate states would have forced the state's hand at some point, or it would have faced invasion and received much more damage in the ensuing war. The "extremists" that fed off of the state's "radical spirit" had won the day, but even so, the state "only grudgingly left the Union to avoid fighting against the South."[18]

On May 20, defeated and discouraged, the conservatives in the legislature joined their opponents and voted unanimously to leave the Union, all 120 signing the bill. North Carolina became the last state to secede (Tennessee seceded on May 7 but didn't have a referendum until the next month).

State senator and future governor Jonathan Worth felt Lincoln had abandoned common sense by calling for troops, which he had to know would get fence-sitting Southerners to fall on the side of secession. All benefit of the doubt allowed Lincoln vanished overnight.

Worth said to a family member, "I think the South is committing suicide, but my lot is cast with the South and being unable to manage the ship, I intend to face the breakers manfully and go down with my companions." Worth felt that if Lincoln had withdrawn the troops at Sumter, which seemed to be what Congress wanted instead of sending the fleet, "this state and Tennessee and the other states which had not passed the ordinance of secession, would have stood up for the Union. . . . All of us who had stood by the Union, felt that he [Lincoln] had abandoned us and had surrendered us to the tender mercies of Democracy & the Devil."[19]

Confederate president Jefferson Davis said that the South only wanted what the "Old Union" promised and that neither he nor the Confederacy had plans to invade the North. The North at first wanted to simply preserve the Union, but after Lincoln began to talk about emancipation in the fall of 1862, without a doubt the conflict became about slavery as well.

With no say, Wright and his family, friends, and neighbors, as well as most citizens of the South, were cast into something in which they had no interest or stake. The wealthy gentry had signed onto a proxy war that would be fought by the lower classes, and the legislature's action did not reflect the will of the people it was supposed to represent. It was a war doomed from the start, flamed by passion, ignorance, immorality, and greed, an event that would set the state, the South, and civil rights back a century in four years of constant death, despair, and destruction.

Many Southerners such as Arrington had grossly overestimated the South and also the world's view. "[The] South [is] able to export upwards of $200 million and can produce everything requisite under lawful duties—sufficient revenue and capital would flow thru if needed." He, along with others, also assumed support from Europe. "Great Britain has never interfered with slavery in Brazil or Cuba . . . would Great Britain allow the Black Republican to blockade Southern ports—she is compelled to have cotton." Davis agreed. There were offers of $600 million in funding from Europe with Southern cotton as security, but Davis felt that no more than $15 million should be taken. He could have sold $50 million in cotton before the blockade became effective, but he withheld it in the hope of using it as a bargaining chip for recognition as a country.[20]

Arrington even went so far as to espouse a view held by many that the North had actually provoked the South into a financial war: "Protection tariff[s] & tonnage duties to protect their shipping . . . the Yankees have outwilled Great Britain . . . raged slavery agitation to dissolve the Union and breakdown her rivals in manufacturing." He added that the South was seceding for the exact opposite reason most history books list: "[the] Southern Confederacy [wants] the same Old Constitution no change of government—seceded to prevent a change."[21]

Arrington mentioned that many in the North also blamed Lincoln for the way the crisis was handled. In a letter where he references a speech, Arrington wrote: "*The New York Herald* felt Lincoln was the most dangerous man that could be elected. They are for the Union with a proviso that is if the Black Republicans will concede to the South all our rights, upon such terms as will bring back all the seceding states and that is all that has been required."[22]

Shortly after July 4, Governor Ellis died of consumption while in office, and the North Carolina Speaker of the House, Henry T. Clark of Edgecombe County, filled out the term, which was the order of succession at the time. As late as 1862 Union sentiment was still strong in the state, which was proven by the election of reluctant secessionist Zebulon Vance later that year. Before the war Vance was assistant editor of the *Asheville Spectator* and was an ardent Unionist. He ran a race for Congress against incumbent Thomas L. Clingman and called him a "liar and scoundrel" for his radical rhetoric and his pro-secession stances. Vance lost the race, but then he gained the seat anyway when Clingman went to the Senate. He later defeated another pro-secession candidate, William W. Avery.[23] The inevitable tide was sweeping in, and most had resigned themselves to what one anonymous man said: "I am a Union man, but when they send men South it will change my notions. I can do nothing against my own people."[24]

5

My Civil War Past

We can only imagine the history of the free world today if,
at the end of the Civil War, there had been two countries: the
United States and the Confederate States of America.

—DOUGLAS BRINKLEY, author and history professor

There was a big, blue, clothbound book at Bailey Elementary School
with the words *The Civil War* printed on the front cover. Just below
that two figures, one sketched in blue, and the other in gray, were
merging into one, crouching for an impending impact, rifle butts
raised sharply, bayonets in mid thrust. From about third grade until
I went to junior high, my name appeared on the checkout card on
the back inside cover more than three or four times; I think only
one other person's name appeared on it the entire time I was there.
I know this because later, when I was in high school, the same volume turned up on Southern Nash Senior High School's discard
pile, and I snatched it up.

The book was slim, and oversized, with that black tape that
libraries used to protect and hold bindings so many years ago. The
cloth-covered cardboard covers were frayed at the corners. The
leaves were thick in my hands. Each page was beautifully illustrated, with accompanying text about the key moments of the war.
On the inside cover was a map of the United States, with all the
states at the time, and more sketches of soldiers showing which
states belonged to the Confederacy and which belonged to the

Union. I studied this book carefully and found it fascinating as it went far beyond the details of our family's World Book Encyclopedia. It has since disappeared from my collection, inadvertently donated or boxed in the attic. I realized only later that it certainly represented the Southern viewpoint, as everything else regarding the war within my fingertips in the 1970s and 1980s did. For many years, long before the internet, it was my main source of information on the War Between the States.

We never came close to talking about the war in grades K–6 and only glanced at it in grades 7–9, mostly in the mandatory North Carolina history class, with the synopsis being "not many battles happened here." Certainly, the phrase "Lost Cause" was romanticized in most of the things I read, but it was rarely identified as anything specific or defined in any tangible way. If anything, the war to me seemed to be about resisting authority even when you couldn't win. The Lost Cause is essentially an interpretation of the Civil War that holds the South in the best possible light, the North in the worst possible light, with Robert E. Lee as the patron saint, and historical accuracy optional, as "many historians have labeled the Lost Cause a myth or a legend." But more on that in chapter 14.

The rest of my school years managed to effectively dodge the Civil War, as well as World War II, Korea, and Vietnam. Honestly, I'm not sure what we covered beyond the ancient Romans and Greeks, the Middle Ages, the Lost Colony, and the New Deal. I read all I could find on my own, and in contrast with the view of many today, the theme was that the war was over states' rights, with slavery being foremost among those rights; most histories available to me were adamant that the war was not fought solely over slavery. Clearly this was a war initiated by a small group of self-minded rich and powerful (and delusional) men who committed many immoralities, the worst of which was upon black men and women, and not the least of which was upon their poor white fellow citizens, whom they disregarded almost as much. To say the war was only about slavery or not about slavery is to be wrong on both accounts. There were clearly white supremacists in the leadership of the Confederacy and among its ranks and its citizenry, but to claim all involved were white supremacists is not truthful. Captain Thorp himself commented on this late in his life in a newspaper interview at a Confederate reunion: "It is regretted that some of our people born since the war believe that if there had been no African slavery there would have been no war between the North and South. This is a sad mistake."[1]

In our playground and backyard games my friends and I sometimes played Civil War, as boys then often played with toy guns without raising eyebrows, taking the high ground with dirt clod grenades and plastic rifles purchased from the dime store. Race never was a part of this game, it was purely regional—Us versus the Yankees. "Yankee" was a pejorative in the 1970s and 1980s in North Carolina—and still is, although certainly thrown with less frequency and hatred today, usually as a counterpunch to insults such as "hick," "redneck," or "hillbilly."

There were few Yankees in Nash County during my childhood, and it seemed when we did encounter them, they talked fast, and often talked down to the natives, and often offered solutions about how things could be done better, like they were "back home." A factory in town that employed many "transplants" was often blamed in overheard conversations during my adolescent years for bringing illegal drugs with them, along with their accents and attitudes. Southern hospitality is one thing, but it does have its limits, at least with outsiders. That courtesy often ends with "Why don't you go back there if it was so great?" or "I-95 has a northbound lane, too." There's also the old joke about the difference between Yankees and Damn Yankees: Yankees visited and went back home, Damn Yankees visited and stayed. Regional rivalries die hard. Today, there seems to be far less animosity as North Carolina's population has boomed this century, bolstered by an influx of people from out of state. The worst that Yankees get charged with this day is usually in regard to exacerbating the political divide, which is certainly not limited to the South.

The most popular show among ten- to thirteen-year-old boys in my day was undoubtedly *The Dukes of Hazzard*. This show was talked about at recess and lunch on Fridays, the day it aired, and then again on Monday, primarily because of the performance of the Duke boys and their orange 1969 Dodge Charger, the General Lee. I don't remember any conversations about the Confederate battle flag painted on the top of the car, only about how fast and how far the car could fly. Oddly enough on the show, paved roads and people of color were in short supply, even though it was supposed to take place in rural Georgia. The story was about two rebellious young cousins who fought local corruption in a Georgia backwater town, liked fast cars and fast women, and had a female cousin who created a fashion form ("Daisy Duke" shorts), as well as a former moonshining uncle who guided them all with homespun wisdom. Every boy in my school watched it.

Racism was in plain sight in those days. I heard the N-word on a daily basis, as it was tossed about everywhere one went, but almost always safely out of earshot of those at whom it was directed. Because I had friends who were black, I was occasionally asked, usually aggressively, if I was a "n——r lover." When I traveled with those same friends to play pickup basketball they'd sometimes get asked, "Why did you bring the cracker/white boy/m——f——." I never heard any black people use the N-word with one exception: black men in our community who were over the age of about sixty would sometimes use it to refer to someone who was "sorry," another way of saying "no account, no good, good for nothing." I never figured out how to respond, and I usually offered a blank stare and said nothing. Race was sometimes joked about in mixed groups, mostly based around stereotypes, and was self-deprecating. Every once in a while someone would cross that never clearly delineated "line," and awkward, sometimes angry, expressions and silence lingered until the subject was changed.

I never saw the Ku Klux Klan in person or locally, but it was on TV from time to time, even in the 1980s. There was a gunfight in Greensboro in 1979, when the Klan and Neo-Nazis clashed with members of the Communist Workers Party, and several people were killed. Some type of Klan "wizard" lived in nearby Johnston County and held rallies from to time to time that got media coverage to publicize his hate group. The images on TV were surreal.

The Klan even had a phone hotline, and it was a popular prank for folks to hand the number out and claim it was the number for a new restaurant, only for the victim of the prank to get an earful of crazy, hate-filled rantings. But on their best days the Klan could only muster enough hoods and robes to make themselves into a foolish, televised public spectacle. Most white people were afraid of the Klan and despised them, but with the exception of the few public figures, no one seemed certain who they were or where they lived. Rumors abounded as to who might have "hoods and robes hidden in their closets."

I did not understand the Klan, and my parents had a hard time explaining it. Mama said they were mean and scary and hated black people. Daddy said they were dumbasses. The Klan claimed to be Christians, but they burned crosses, which added to my confusion. Why would a Christian burn the symbol of the salvation sacrifice of Jesus? Simply to "illuminate" the night? That was as much nonsense as claiming to follow a religion that clearly states "love one another," with no exceptions listed, and in the next breath calling for harm to another person based on the color of his or her skin. Nothing they said jived with church or the Bible, especially when they spewed hatred toward Jews as well. On the other hand I surely did hear "church-going folks" say "n——r" on a regular basis. We've taught our children that the N-word is a curse word, as I think most people my age have, and it recently occurred to me that they might be part of the first generation of white Southerners to come along that has never uttered the word. After hearing "n——r" so much over the course of my life, knowing how it was meant, it makes me uncomfortable today when I hear young black students use it, with or without the r. We'd all be better served if it faded from the nation's collective vocabulary.

For me, the outcome of the Civil War was never really considered; it was a moment in history, long settled, and I loved history and its stories. That the South's generals were brilliant but outnumbered was a theme of my early readings. My view was somewhat limited. That changed with two things: I met my future wife, and I took a history class at Barton College titled "The Civil War."

Kristi is from near the Shenandoah Valley and grew up within a short drive of Culpeper, Chancellorsville, Fredericksburg, Orange, Brandy Station, the Wilderness, Spotsylvania Courthouse, and many other places that I'd seen in books all my life. While we were dating, we took the college class together, which was taught by a brilliant professor named Ed Holloway, a Damn Yankee from Connecticut. Holloway presented the Civil War from a crazy new viewpoint: the unvarnished truth and all the ugliness of both sides, the ignorance of the whole idea, the incompetence and fallibilities of those who conducted the war, and the long-lasting effect it had on this country and continues to have. He didn't hesitate to highlight the many mistakes of Robert E. Lee, the incompetence of Jefferson Davis, and the sheer lunacy of the whole ordeal, and he gave just as much time to the wrongs committed by the North. He examined and presented the war as history but with scorn for many of the participants. It ended any notion of a "glorious CSA." The heroes and villains were humanized, and the often inaccurate stories were clarified and given context. This was new territory, and it changed my way of thinking about history forever.

Kristi and I visited those battlefields many times, and each time they offered a little more reality, and a little less glory. Virginia has done a wonderful job of saving its historic sites, although ground has been lost to developers over time. I'll never forget the first time I saw Wilderness and Chancellorsville, the rolling hills, the beautiful mountain backdrop, the cannon used to mark lines, along with wooden fences. I tried to imagine the sweat and fear and intensity of being close enough for men on each side to see fellow countrymen face-to-face and fire into them. A four-year bloodbath. We took in how many lives were lost, how the direction of a people was changed, and how a generation of Americans was wiped out—it became harder and harder to fathom, especially when reading names and not just numbers on casualty lists. Kristi, now a research historian, was into genealogy as well, and the seeds of this book were planted during those explorations into family trees.

What were some of those other solutions? What happens when you read history not as a foregone conclusion but as a series of problems and alternative outcomes? Would Lincoln's buyout plan for slaves been much like the tobacco allotment program for tobacco? But wait: this was people, not a crop; slaves were considered property first, then human, subhuman, or inferior beings next. Certainly there would have been resistance, and violence, and resentment, especially by poor whites who would suddenly have millions of competitors for low-level jobs. The suffering of blacks might not have been lessened at all. At some point, I wondered, how do other countries see our Civil War? How do they see the internal bickering that continues to this day?

I realized that throughout my childhood I'd given no thought to the blessing it was, the miracle, that the South lost the war. This seemed almost treasonous when it first descended on me, and certainly it would have drawn the scorn of many of the folks in our community had I mentioned this blasphemy in the 1970s. How was it not obvious that this great country could never have been two great countries, or that slavery would have caused the physical destruction of the continent as it was causing the moral one? Sci-fi/ fantasy author Harry Turtledove laid this out in several works in the 1990s, including *Guns of the South, How Few Remain*, and the Great War and the American Empire trilogies, all books I devoured. These alternative histories are terrifying to anyone who loves this country. Historical fiction by Michael and Jeff Shaara made true-life events more vivid with the personable treatment of well-known figures in *Killer Angels, Gods and Generals*, and *The Last Full Measure*. Perhaps no New South perspective is better than Tony Horwitz's *Confederates in the Attic*.

I like to think that preservation of the United States, the country that would eventually stretch from sea to shining sea, that saved Europe and Asia from total destruction, that produced the telephone, the television, space flight, central air-conditioning, Humphrey Bogart, Larry Bird, Carl Yastrzemski, Martin Luther King, Teddy Roosevelt, Dwight Eisenhower, Langston Hughes, Ernest Hemingway, and Susan B. Anthony, would have trumped any argument to put on gray and go to war. Forced to choose, surely I would have headed north and supported my country. But then I realize that is how my twenty-first-century self thinks. This presentism, or an attitude toward the past dominated by present-day attitudes and experiences, creates my divided self. In a time where many considered their loyalty to be to their state first, that it was their "true" country, could I have taken up arms against my neighbors, forfeited my property, left my family behind at the mercy of whatever befell them? Hindsight may say side with the Union, but in the immediacy of the times I feel certain there would have been little choice beyond service to the Confederacy. There are no simple answers when it comes to the Civil War, perhaps our most complicated and complex era.

I can drive just a few miles in any direction from my house and see a Confederate battle flag in a yard. But what can the homeowners tell me about the flag or the war? Do they know it is a battle flag or do they think it is "the Confederate flag?" (The flag most people identify as the confederate flag was used to identify units in the war; the actual, official confederate flag was different, it had a blue field like the U.S. flag, with two wide red stripes spilt by a parallel wide white stripe.) Are they white supremacists? Racists? Do they know or care that it likely casts them into a certain stereotype, that their African American neighbors may resent it? Do they have an interest in history or ancestors who fought in the Civil War? Is it just a sign of rebellion? All my life I've seen the battle flag used as promos for beer companies and rock bands and on T-shirts, license plates, bumper stickers, beach towels, and baseball caps. I didn't see it as offensive, but that's just my perspective. Should I have seen it this way? Were my friends afraid to say something, or was it not on their minds?

Upon deeper reflection, I think I would probably have been much like Wright Stephen Batchelor. The notion of an independent association of independent states would have seemed acceptable to someone living in the most rural of areas. Regardless of previous standoffs, once the soldiers in blue invaded the South, defending my home would not have been a romantic thought as much as it would have been a practical one, a means of survival. Rural eastern North Carolinians were survivors who lived hard lives in hard times. Limited travel made people from north of the Mason-Dixon Line seem like foreigners. There was not much choice in whether to join the army of the Cause. Geography, economics, and commonsense survival drove many in the state to take up support for the Confederacy, and many others were whipped into a frenzy by those who stood to gain the most from Southern independence, and who could not understand the folly of what they wanted, yet managed to justify what they were doing. When war became inevitable, the frenzy among the "true believers" in the Southern cause made opposition dangerous for those who spoke against the csa or did not want to serve in the army; consequences could include beatings or destruction of property. The intellectual divide is remarkable in hindsight. If I could not read or write, I would have had less interest in policy, and far more on survival. Perhaps lost in today's great debate on the Civil War is the willingness to put ourselves truly in the shoes of those who lived in the times, not with our knowledge now but with their knowledge then.

North Carolina stands as a paradox when studying the conflict. My state wanted no part of a war. My state supplied more troops, took more casualties, and had relatively few slaveholders. While it can't be said that North Carolina supported the plight of the Negro or any noble notions of every man being created equal, they also did not want to pick a fight. The common man who had no slaves— such as Wright Batchelor—would most likely have been less interested to the politics and social constructs, and more concerned with getting through the next winter.

This of course, brings me to consider my ancestor. I never heard him mentioned by anyone in my family. Was it because he put on a Union uniform? Was it because he deserted? Was it because of his apparent politics after the war? This is so odd in a family where family is so important, but it is yet another paradox perhaps of life in the South. While family is important, it seems a relatively small number of people have interest in learning about their ancestors. Interest in genealogy has grown tremendously over the years with such websites as ancestry.com and DNA testing for origins being more convenient and exciting than digging through musty records in cramped government offices. However, it still only appeals to a small percentage of the population, and most people can't name relatives back more than a couple of generations.

I'm pro-history, but that means all of it—the ugly and the uncomfortable. I'm anti-revisionist but also anti-propagandist. I'm mixed on the monuments and the flag, and believe it is all about context. I'm anti–Confederate flag in public spaces (unless in museums or at historic sites) and pro-flag on private property (people fly flags from other countries all the time, and it is free expression, pleasant or not). I think monuments depend on the who and the where. Some should be moved, and some not.

The Civil War is just as complicated now as the day it started.

6

Wright's Enlistment and Early Campaigns

Any people, anywhere, being inclined and having the
power, have the right to rise up and shake off the existing
government, and form a new one that suits them better. This is a
most valuable, a most sacred right, a right which we hope
and believe is to liberate the world.

—ABRAHAM LINCOLN, U.S. Congress, 1847

There were many paradoxes in the state, no better illustration than former legislator, congressman, future governor, and senator Zebulon Vance of Rowan County. Vance, a staunch Unionist who lobbied loudly against secession and revolt, did an about-face once South Carolina made its move. Always savvy politically, he formed a company of "Rough and Ready Guards" in Raleigh and served as captain, weeks before the state officially seceded. When Fort Sumter fell, he had this say: "For myself, I will say that I was canvassing for the Union with all my strength; I was addressing a large and excited crowd, large numbers of whom were armed, and literally had my arms extended upward in pleading for peace and the Union of our Fathers, when the telegraphic news was announced of the firing on Sumter and [the] President's call for seventy-five thousand volunteers. When my hand came down from that impassioned gesticulation, it fell slowly and sadly by the side of a Secessionist."[1]

By June Vance's unit was in service in Virginia as Company F of the Fourteenth North Carolina Regiment, and by August Vance was colonel of the Twenty-Sixth North Carolina Regiment. However, for Wright and many of the other reluctant North Carolinians, running off to war was no priority. Many common whites, and for that matter all classes, thought the whole disagreement would be worked out without additional gunfire. War was so far removed from the generation that most viewed it as honorable and glorious. The last combat veteran among the Batchelors was Wright's namesake, an uncle who fought in the War of 1812. Those who depended on their farms and the labor of their own hands and their families had no such delusions or aspirations of gallantry.

Many Nash County men such as Wright sat out the entire first year of the conflict, although men from neighboring Edgecombe County quickly formed a regiment and jumped into the fire in the Battle of Bethel, Virginia, in early June 1861. A Tarboro boy, Henry Lawson Wyatt, nineteen, of the First North Carolina Regiment, Company A "Edgecombe Guards," was by most accounts the first Confederate soldier to die in combat, when a Union sharpshooter marked him as he and two others tried to charge across a field to disperse Federals from a house. John H. Thorp of Rocky Mount, who would later become a commanding officer and a friend of Wright's, was wounded in the attack. Along with George T. Williams, Thomas Fallon, Robert Bradley, and Wyatt, Thorp and his comrades became known for the rest of their lives as the "Bethel Heroes."

The attitude for many North Carolinians toward Lincoln changed quite a bit after Bethel. In a letter to his cousin Sallie, Thorp was clear in his feelings toward the president and the enveloping conflict:

> I almost boil when I think of their demon-like chief. (I will not write his infamous name.) In my mind, he is a tyrant of blackest hue, whose base ambition is to be the man who deluged our once happy America in brothers blood. He is too, the veriest fool (pardon me for the expression) that lives. Why what can he do towards conquering us—his avowed purpose—but since he can't be told just let us be backed by the encouragement of our loves who we've left at home and we'll defend them though it be necessary to surround them by trenches of human blood.[2]

The war moved slow but steady. Less than two weeks after Bethel, part of Virginia seceded from the seceded Virginia to rejoin the Union as West Virginia. In July the uss *Daylight* was sent to Wilmington, North Carolina's main port, and one of the key shipping centers of the South, to start the blockade, and a week after that Union forces were routed at the first Battle of Manassas (also known as Bull Run; Southerners used the names of towns in naming battles, while Northerners used nearby bodies of water). That victory gave a false sense of hope to the Confederacy, while making the Union realize this was not going to be a ninety-day insurrection.

In late July President Lincoln replaced Gen. Irwin McDowell with Gen. George McClellan, starting a merry-go-round of leadership that would continue for a good portion of the war. The first income tax to fund the war came right after.

Union troops wasted no time in bringing the fight to the reluctant secessionists and landed at Cape Hatteras, North Carolina, on August 27, 1861, about 150 miles east of Nash County. By November a convention of pro-Union delegates met and appointed Marble Nash Taylor as provisional governor, further dividing the state. Offering little to no resistance was another of the tactical mistakes of the Confederates, as President Jefferson Davis did little to nothing to defend the North Carolina coast, instead diverting almost all resources to Virginia.

Wright Batchelor could certainly be considered an everyman North Carolinian, the perfect metaphor for the state as a whole. He just wanted to be left alone. He wanted no part of a fight, but when he was finally faced with no choice, he did what he had to do.

Wright enlisted in nearby Spring Hope on February 4, 1862, becoming a private at the age of thirty-three. His brother Ruffin, thirty-one, signed up on February 10. It was nearly a year after Fort Sumter was attacked, well after the First Battle of Bull Run, and nine months after North Carolina became the last state to secede before the war finally reached the back roads of Nash County. Perhaps Wright and Ruffin and the other men of the county had gotten wind of an impending draft and knew their odds of sticking together and fighting alongside men they knew and trusted were greater if they enlisted. The Conscription Act was passed in April and required three years of service for all able-bodied men aged eighteen to thirty-five. However, many men, especially those young and eager to prove themselves brave, were swept up into the ranks in a wave of enlistment in county seat Nashville during the last week of February. One recruiting poster promised that a "$100 bounty will be paid to each man as soon as mustered into service; plenty to eat and good clothes will be furnished by the Government. Men who come and bring their horses will be paid 24 dollars per month. Those who have good shot guns can get a good price for them." Very few Nash County men had seen military service, and fewer still had been to war. They were also poor. Of the original 151 men that would ultimately form Wright's company, only 13 had any interest in slave property. Later in the year other incentives were offered as noted by another Nash County veteran, John Wesley Bone of the Thirtieth North Carolina Regiment, who lived outside of Nashville near the Sandy Cross community. After the war Bone said that men were offered $50 and a thirty-day furlough as the government was "realizing that now was the time to get the men into it before they learned the realities of the war."[3]

Wright and the other Nash County men were sent to Raleigh to train at Camp Mangum, leaving behind wives and families. They were soon formed into Company A of the Forty-Seventh Regiment of North Carolina Troops, to be known as the Chicora Guards. It was organized on March 24, 1862. From the 1,200 men in the capital, ten companies were formed. The selection of "Chicora" by Company A remains lost to history; the name referred to a legendary Indian tribe from South Carolina, which, perhaps ironically, had several members sold into slavery by the Spanish. Companies B, C, G, I, and J did not have nicknames, but Company D, also mostly Nash County men, called themselves the Castalia Invincibles, after a community a couple of miles west of Nashville (they were the basis for an alternative history novel titled Guns of the South). Company F, primarily men from neighboring Franklin County, were called the Sons of Liberty, Company H was the North Carolina Tigers, and Company K was the Alamance Minute Men.

Days after Wright's enlistment, Union general Ambrose Burnside attacked Roanoke Island, and by February 12 Edenton, less than seventy miles inland on the Albemarle Sound, had fallen. In the west, Nashville, Tennessee, was taken on February 24. The Merrimack and the Monitor clashed on March 9, and four days later the war moved closer to Nash County. McClellan was removed to the Army of the Potomac on March 11, and Burnside continued his push from the coast, landing troops on the west branch of the Neuse River at New Bern. New Bern, the former capital, was the second oldest town in North Carolina and a center of wealth once known as "The Athens of the South." At one time it was the largest city, was a center of trade, and was an area with a lot of slaves (it is widely believed that over ten thousand slaves escaped from New Bern during the war).

New Bern was taken on March 14. The siege of Fort Macon, on the coast near Morehead City, began in earnest on March 23. Some of the recruits from Camp Mangum were rushed to Kinston to protect the city, but in the ultimate foreshadowing of how things might follow, they were not issued firearms. They returned to Raleigh within two weeks to continue drilling.

Maj. Sion Rogers of Raleigh became colonel and was joined by Lt. Col. George H. Faribault and Maj. John A. Graves as the top commanders. Other officers included Capts. Archibald Crudup, John W. Bryant, and John H. Thorp and Lts. George W. Westray, Wilson Baily, Sidney Bridgers, Thomas Westray, and later Benjamin H. Bunn. Years after the war, Thorp authored a beautifully written regimental history, as well as an accounting for all those who served in the Forty-Seventh Regiment.

Thorp was a key leader and trusted member of the officer corps in the Forty-Seventh. A schoolteacher, he'd enlisted in the Edgecombe Guards in April 1861 at age twenty, just a year after graduating from the University of North Carolina. After the Battle of Bethel he left the unit to help form the Forty-Seventh and Company A. During the war, Thorp declined promotion on more than one occasion to remain a captain so he could stay with his men and lead the company.

Camp Mangum became a beehive of activity, and Thorp wrote that the men were "drilled incessantly" by Gen. James G. Martin, a West Point graduate from Elizabeth City, a riverfront town in the northeast corner of the state bordering the Great Dismal Swamp. (Martin would later surrender the last organized Confederate army in the state from his posting in western North Carolina, at Waynesville.) Various groups were shuttled between Raleigh and the New Bern/ Kinston area to counter Union movements before a "sick period" set in. Sanitation was poor in camps and hospitals, and disease wracked both sides and took disproportionate casualties throughout the war. Flies were everywhere; many men would not bathe, and most men did not know how to cook, wash, or sew. The state fell well short of providing the necessary equipment, food, and arms. In close quarters for the first time in their lives, many had trouble adjusting to camp life. Measles, mumps, and malaria tore through the recruits, and the Forty-Seventh wasn't spared. Bryant, forty, a former justice of the peace, died on June 25, 1862, back in Nash County (after being sent home), and Baily eventually passed away as well. Bryant, well regarded, left behind a wife and four children. Thorp wrote that "very few escaped sickness." Typhoid fever or "camp fever" was rampant and caused by a type of salmonella bacteria in contaminated water or food. It brought on flu-like symptoms and often led to sepsis, cardiac failure, peritonitis, pneumonia, or life-threatening intestinal disease.[4]

In addition, camp life was a rough adjustment for many men, who had spent most of their daily life somewhat in isolation on their farms and were now exposed to crowded life with many different personalities and with cursing, sometimes vulgar and hard-drinking comrades surrounding them. The air was heavy with flies and sickness amid the infamous heat and humidity of a North Carolina summer. As bad as it was, the soldiers would eventually long for their time in Raleigh, as John W. Bone later recalled: "We were having a very good time here [Camp Mangum], but did not realize it, though we did later on."[5]

The typical soldier carried an 1853 Enfield rifle that fired a .577 caliber bullet, unless he had supplied his own firearm. Usually, forty to sixty rounds were carried in a cartridge box. Most soldiers had knives and a bayonet, although many men on both sides refused to use the bayonet, even in close fighting. Rations included hardtack, sometimes beef, cornmeal, and, when they could get it, coffee. Confederates usually had an eight-ounce wooden canteen with a cork stopper. Other items in the pack might include pipes, tobacco, paper, a pencil, plates and utensils, tin cups, diaries, Bibles, razors, brushes, combs, candles, watches, socks, needle and thread, and possibly playing cards, dice, dominoes, or even musical instruments.[6] As the war dragged on, the packs got lighter and lighter as items were lost, discarded, destroyed, or no longer available.

Public support was stirred as civilians and news outlets alike began to feel their braggadocio. When giving a report of elected officers in the regiments at camp, the *Semi-Weekly State Journal* couldn't resist this bit of trash talk at the end of the list, in its April 5 edition: "North Carolina will send her full quota to the field, and have a home reserve that will astonish her sister States, and may yet give Burnside and his mob of negro-stealing, grave-robbers considerable trouble. Every man and every dollar for the war, and death to our thievish invaders is the rallying cry of the Old North State."[7]

Disaster struck the Confederates on April 6 when Gen. Albert Sidney Johnston was killed at Shiloh, and General Grant's reinforced and larger army managed to push replacement Gen. P. G. T. Beauregard from the field. It was the bloodiest day in American history at that point—although the war would see to it that the record fell several more times—with twenty-three thousand combined casualties from both sides. Fort Macon surrendered on April 25, the same day that Union admiral David Farragut damned the torpedoes and took New Orleans in the western theater of operations.

The Forty-Seventh soon tired of the monotony of drill, especially with Virginia so close, and so full of action, with mostly Confederate successes. It was a common belief on both sides that the war would quickly end, and soldiers in their naïveté did not want to miss the action, best put by Thorp that the desire was to go to "scenes being enacted around Richmond . . . [but] . . . [t]he boon is not yet granted us."[8] On April 11, six of the ten companies in the Forty-Seventh were mustered into service, with three more following on April 29 and the last on April 30. They were transferred to the Confederate States of America (csa) for three years' service the next month.

The regiment got its wish in July when it was sent to Drewery's Bluff on the James River outside of Richmond to reinforce a position that had been defended there in the battle in mid-May. With no action forthcoming, the Forty-Seventh was then posted as the provost guard in Petersburg and to protect the Petersburg and Weldon and the Wilmington and Weldon Railroads, where they established a good relationship with the citizens and reported "no unpleasant incidents." In May they were sent into camp between Kinston and New Bern, where they continued to drill until July when they returned to Petersburg to brigade with the Forty-Fourth and the Fifty-Second North Carolina Regiments under General Martin. While the Forty-Seventh did not stay in the area long enough to participate in the Battle of Malvern Hill in July, many residents of Nash County claimed to have heard the cannon fire from that engagement—which was 160 miles away.[9]

Shuttling from Eastern North Carolina to Virginia

The war continued to rage without the Forty-Seventh. Confederate general Thomas "Stonewall" Jackson won at Front Royal and Winchester, Virginia, but a week later the Union retook Front Royal in May. In June rebel general J. E. B. Stuart went on his famous ride around McClellan's army, and the Seven Days Campaign began, ending with a Union victory at Malvern Hill, but Richmond remained safe. August saw the Second Battle of Manassas (Bull Run), and September saw the bloodiest day of the war during the Battle of Sharpsburg (Antietam). In early November President Lincoln replaced McClellan with Gen. Ambrose Burnside. General Lee won at Fredericksburg, Virginia, on December 13.

Movement by Union troops under Gen. John G. Foster in New Bern saw the men of the Forty-Seventh moved to Weldon in early November, just in time for an uncharacteristic snowstorm that dropped six inches of snow. Thorp noted the only cover was "bark, boughs, and dirt," and small brandy rations were issued for warmth. It was a brief, bitter cold stay. In December the Forty-Seventh found itself back in Petersburg, camped near the Twenty-Sixth North Carolina and within five miles of the city. The Forty-Seventh was the only regiment with a hospital set up and was regarded as clean, with good books kept during inspection.

General Foster again posed a threat, this time to Kinston, and on December 14 Company A and the rest of the Forty-Seventh was put on a train. When they arrived after dark, Confederate commander Gen. Nathan G. Evans was retreating across a bridge over the Neuse River. Wright and his fellow infantrymen were unloaded, and the train chugged away, in what must have been an ominous feeling of impending combat and abandonment. Such was the chaos that Colonel Rogers formed lines and went double-quick to cover Evans's retreat. Men were told to pile knapsacks, overcoats, and blankets near the tracks, which proved to be another debacle as Thorp recorded of the matériel, "We never heard of afterwards."

Foster sent a message demanding surrender, and Evans halted his retreat to respond, "Tell General Foster I will fight him here." Foster, like a number of his colleagues in the Virginia campaign, was hesitant to engage and decided not to pursue, and Evans retreated to Falling Creek, an area that today lies between Kinston and Goldsboro on Highway 70, a well-traveled route to the North Carolina beaches.

The next day Company A reconnoitered a two-mile stretch toward Kinston but could not find the enemy. Along with Company K, they later found Foster had advanced up the south bank of the Neuse. Foster tried to cross the water at White Hall but was stopped, and then he continued his march toward Goldsboro, with the Forty-Seventh in pursuit. The men marched across a county bridge and formed a line of battle, planning to attack the next morning after shivering through the cold, late December night. When they awoke the next morning, they found Foster had once again chosen not to fight and had retreated.

The Forty-Seventh was sent with the Fifty-Second to the Blackwater River, which flows from Virginia across the North Carolina border into the Chowan River near Elizabeth City. They were placed under Gen. Roger Pryor of Virginia to protect southeastern Virginia. Wright and his fellow privates marched thirty miles a day, constantly on the verge on an engagement or pending battle, falling into a series of skirmishes, and alternating between retreating and advancing. The regiment marched from Garysburg, North Carolina, a stop on the Petersburg Railroad, south to Rocky Mount, North Carolina, where Gen. James J. Pettigrew set up his winter headquarters on January 5, 1863, and the Forty-Fourth joined them. The main goal was to prevent any more raids to the area like the Foster fiasco. Being in their home county, many men of the Forty-Seventh applied for leave as they felt the campaigns were over for the winter. Desertions were up due to the Conscription Act, and it is unknown how many leave applications were granted. It's likely many men, including Wright, got to see their families. For some it would be the last time for years, and for some it would simply be the last time. The war would not be distant much longer. Without much else going on, the men occupied themselves with baseball and went to church, mostly to become acquainted with the area's unmarried women. There wasn't much to do in camp, and conversation topics included incompetent superiors, the draft, poor rations and quantity of rations (the men spent more time trying to feed themselves than fighting), their fellow soldiers, and politics.[10]

January 1863 saw changes. Colonel Rogers was elected attorney general of North Carolina, and the other officers all moved up. The Forty-Seventh was then brigaded with the North Carolina Eleventh, Twenty-Sixth, Forty-Fourth, and Fifty-Second Regiments under Gen. James Johnston Pettigrew of Tyrell County, who had already achieved legendary status. Pettigrew was a University of North Carolina graduate, a valedictorian at age sixteen, and a well-educated man who had been a professor, a lawyer, a legislator from South Carolina (where he had moved), who had spent two years in Europe, and who spoke five languages.[11] Despite his scholarly appearance and bearing, he showed no reluctance to fight. Pettigrew was severely injured in the throat, windpipe, and shoulder in the Battle of Seven Pines in the summer of 1862. He believed he was dying and would not let his men remove him from the field, even after taking another bullet wound and being bayoneted in the leg. He passed out and was captured by Union soldiers, but he was exchanged two days later. This North Carolina command was his first after recovering from his wounds the previous fall. After Goldsboro, to prevent stragglers and deserters, Pettigrew ordered that anyone who left the ranks was to be bayoneted, and that he wanted all ammo salvaged from the dead after battle.

They joined up with Gen. D. H. Hill's army to move on New Bern. In the middle of March a forced march by the Forty-Seventh ended in an early dawn attack, and the Confederates drove Union pickets past a block house. But, Thorp noted in his history, "by failure of other troops to cooperate, time was lost," and an enemy gunboat opened up and shelled the brigade. Pettigrew was unable to respond with his cannon and couldn't cross with the infantry, so he was forced to withdraw, amazingly with no casualties reported.

The force then went to Greenville and Washington and crossed the Tar River in canoes in high water, which caused enough chaos to draw the attention of Union gunboats when the men were close enough to threaten Washington. One man was killed and several wounded. At this point the men resigned themselves to gathering supplies. The plan was abandoned on April 15.

Further north, Lee reorganized his army and was making preparations for a second invasion of the North. Pettigrew's brigade was sent to join Gen. Henry Heth's division in Gen. A. P. Hill's Third Corps, thus enjoining Wright, Company A, and the Forty-Seventh to the Army of Northern Virginia. Hill had taken command of the division after Stonewall Jackson was killed at the Battle of Chancellorsville in May 1863. Hill, from Culpepper, Virginia, had distinguished himself at the Seven Days' Battle, Cedar Mountain, Second Manassas (Bull Run), Sharpsburg (Antietam), and Fredericksburg. Hill had a long-running feud with Jackson and had been arrested, and Jackson pressed Lee for a court martial. Lee managed to put it off because he valued both Jackson and Hill, and it only ended because Jackson died. Hill was wounded at Chancellorsville and was still recovering. While moving north, a train accident between Goldsboro and Halifax happened when a train carrying the Eleventh rammed into a train carrying the Twenty-Sixth, which had stopped to let a mail train pass. Casualties were few, but it was upsetting for the men. The Forty-Seventh was the last of the brigade to leave North Carolina, sitting idle for two weeks between Kinston and Greenville while the rest of the units guarded the supply line at Hanover Junction. On May 1 they were sent to Richmond to protect the Richmond, Fredericksburg and Potomac Railroad and the bridges over the North Anna and South Anna Rivers.

In early June, the men marched to Fredericksburg, where some of them broke the rules and traded tobacco for coffee with Yankee pickets. They saw the destruction of war as they passed through Chancellorsville on June 16, tramping over and around torn up trees, dead horses, and bodies in shallow graves, partially exposed. From there they went to Culpepper Courthouse in the shadow of the Blue Ridge Mountains, through Winchester, and crossed the Potomac at Shepherdstown, West Virginia, on June 24. At this point Pettigrew issued warnings against interfering with local famers and towns-people, as the Confederates hoped to win over the many sympa-thizers with not just military force but with good public relations.

Around June 25 they moved through the Sharpsburg battlefield, at last being exposed to the horrors of the war, which they had so longed to join as they slogged around in North Carolina, mostly chasing Yankee shadows. They had not seen real combat, nor were they prepared for it. This made their movements all the more somber. Thorp hinted at temptation as the Forty-Seventh marched through Hagerstown, Maryland, referring to it as "opulent," but there was no looting. By June 29 the men were in Pennsylvania and camped near Cashtown, eight miles west of a small town called Gettysburg. Despite orders, men were taking chickens and vegetables along the march to supplement the insufficient rations.

All of them, generals down to privates, were on the verge of becoming part of history. The Forty-Seventh's first real action would take place at the impending battle that was the watershed of the war. Not only would they become initiated into the fire and brim-stone hell of war, but key moments and history debates that continue to this day would spider from this upcoming three-day span. Wright would find himself a long way from home and facing his first real test of survival: the Battle of Gettysburg.

7

Bloodbaths at Gettysburg and Bristoe Station

War loses a great deal of romance after a soldier has seen his
first battle. I have a more vivid recollection of the first than the
last one I was in. It is a classical maxim that it is sweet and
becoming to die for one's country; but whoever has seen the
horrors of a battle-field feels that it is far sweeter to live for it.

—Col. JOHN S. MOSBY, *Mosby's War Reminiscences*

Gettysburg, Minus Day 1

On June 30, 1863, Confederate general A. P. Hill's corps marched
toward Gettysburg as a light rain fell all day, not looking for a fight
but moving toward one. Some accounts tell that Hill was out to find
shoes at a factory there, as many of the Confederates were bare-
footed. However, other historians have written that previous rebel
scouting missions would have already revealed such supplies didn't
exist. Their encounter with Union troops on this date led to much
criticism of Hill after the war, including blaming him for the loss
at Gettysburg by engaging before Lee had all his forces in place.

General Heth ordered Pettigrew to recon Gettysburg but not to
engage the enemy. There were reports that just a few militia were
posted around the town. The men mustered for pay and were then
told to leave their knapsacks behind. Men of the Eleventh, Twenty-
Sixth, and Forty-Seventh Regiments moved out at 6 a.m.

Along the way, Pettigrew met up with the Fifty-Fifth Virginia and
asked them to come along since they had been in the area already.

The men stopped at Seminary Ridge, about three-quarters of a mile from town, at 9:30 a.m. and sent out skirmishers. After an hour they saw the head of a Union cavalry unit belonging to Gen. John Buford's division riding toward Gettysburg. They sent word to Heth, but he refused to believe any substantial Union force was close. Pettigrew has been criticized by some for not engaging, and while doing so would have possibly convinced his superiors that a larger Union force was approaching, it would have been a clear disobedience of orders, and that was not Pettigrew's choice. The back-and-forth, cat-and-mouse action the brigade had seen in eastern North Carolina and Virginia had done little to get them combat ready, and that inexperience would prove costly.

As Company A neared Gettysburg, a person dressed as a civilian on a farm horse rode out from the woods and asked to speak to the commander. The officers were immediately suspicious, and the man was quickly questioned to ascertain whether he was a spy. The rider suddenly took off, and the Confederates were fired on from both sides of the road—they had walked into an ambush. Lt. J. Rowan Rogers, brother of Sion Rogers, of Company I reported that Colonel Faribault ordered Company A and Company C to take five men each and attack. The blue coats quickly retreated with little damage. It was a bug swatting compared to what was to come.

The brigade stopped at Marsh Creek, about four miles from Gettysburg, with a regiment on each side of the road, and a third straddling it. After two hours they left the Twenty-Sixth at Marsh Creek, and the Eleventh and Forty-Seventh camped between McKnightstown and Seven Stars.

Reports don't specify who the men from Company A were who chased the bushwhackers, but it is possible that Wright was among them. Regardless, tensions were high in the camp that night. The men had fired at an enemy they couldn't see and ran them off, but how far? How many awaited them the next day? Wright and his fellow privates had trouble tamping down the adrenaline under the clear Pennsylvania night, stars aglow, the heat lingering from a midsummer's day. As they slept, they had no idea what was just before them.

Gettysburg, Day 1

On July 1 General Heth picked up Pettigrew's brigade at 7 a.m. on a hot and humid morning. Company A had eighty-two men on its roster reported as fit for duty, each armed with forty rounds of ammunition. Morale was "splendid," according to Thorp. They were put in Heth's line between Gen. James J. Archer and Col. J. M. Brockenbough.

Between Marsh Creek and Herr's Ridge the column was fired on by Union pickets hidden in the woods. Company C took fifty men to the right and Company A took fifty men to the left to drive off the attackers, with Wright most likely among them as one of the most experienced men. They forced the Yankees into retreat and held off more skirmishers as the Twenty-Sixth and Eleventh advanced on toward Gettysburg. Wright and the rest of the Forty-Seventh filed in behind them.

About two and a half miles from town the North Carolina men were deployed on open ground and took artillery rounds for half an hour. They moved half a mile to the top of Herr's Ridge and stopped in a "skirt of woods," which was bordered by a fence. They took a position in the trees and could see across Willoughby Run and a wheat field that stood between them and the enemy. The skirmishers fired for two hours at Companies G and K of the Eightieth New York, known as the Iron Brigade, and the Forty-Seventh took some casualties.

Pettigrew had nearly 2,600 men to Maj. Gen. Abner Doubleday's 1,361, but the Eightieth had far more combat experience. The Forty-Seventh had 353 men combined with 567 of the Fifty-Second to make their attack. The order finally came at three o'clock.

Company A and the rest of the Forty-Seventh were part of the first charge and were met with a furious storm of shell and canister as well as the rifle fire of two army corps. After the first artillery round gashed the lines, the ranks were closed. The men were quiet as they delivered steady fire, when suddenly they broke into rebel yells as they closed on the first Union line. A frantic struggle ensued, and the line yielded into the second, which was quickly broken by the North Carolinians.

Capt. John D. S. Cooke of the Eightieth New York later described the advance of the Forty-Seventh this way:

> From the forest in front appeared a long brown line of the enemy's infantry. In poetry and romance the Confederate uniform is gray. In actual service it was a butternut brown, and on those fellows who faced us at short range was, owing to their long campaign, as dirty, disreputable and unromantic as can well be imagined. They exhibited no more of "the pomp and circumstance of glorious war" than so many railroad section hands. But they could shoot all right and they stood out there in line in the open field and poured in a rapid fire of musketry they gave us no time to criticize their appearance.[1]

The sun was blistering those on the battlefield, and men were so hot and soaked with sweat in their wool uniforms that they were having trouble ramming down cartridges and handling powder. They had so much trouble with the slick ramrods that "all expedients were resorted to," and many of them jabbed the rods against the ground and rocks strewn across the field, desperate to reload, the survival instinct pushing a frantic pace. They sought targets through the hazy smoke. The infantrymen lost sight of additional Union troops as they pressed across fields of wheat that headed at "breast high."[2]

Suddenly men in blue rose out of the wheat, less than half a football field away, as if they'd been awakened from a deep sleep, surprised. Thorp described the scene, as the Yankees returned fire: "When suddenly a third line of the enemy arose forty yards in front as if by magic, and leveled their shining line of gun barrels on the wheat heads. Though taken by surprise the roar of our guns sounded along our whole line. We had caught the drop on them . . . [but then] . . . the earth just seemed to open up and take that line, which five minutes ago was so perfect."[3]

Just as the line crumbled, one of the oddities of war took place, surreal and with the odd emotion that so often followed up-close combat. A mounted Union officer, Col. Chapman Biddle of Philadelphia, rallied his Pennsylvania troops, and a mass of soldiers moved on the men of the Forty-Seventh. Just as the opposing troops closed, they were gone in a flash, as a Confederate gun raked them to pieces. Thorp noted that when his men heard afterward that Biddle had survived the shelling, they were happy, glad to know the hero, their enemy, had made it through. Wright and the men would have seen the whole episode unfold as Thorp described: "The scattered Federals swarmed around him [Biddle] as bees cover their queen. . . . In the midst of a heterogeneous mass of men, . . . he approached our left when all guns in front and from right and left turned on the mass and seemingly shot the whole to pieces."[4] Biddle survived but was wounded later in the day.

As the North Carolina troops headed toward McPherson's Ridge, about seventy-five yards out they could see the 80th New York and the 142nd Pennsylvania just behind. While the 47th and 52nd were having success, the 11th and 26th were getting "cut to pieces," one man from the 47th later said. The brigade had 1,100 killed or wounded, while the 47th took about 125 casualties. Heth was wounded, and Pettigrew took over command. Company C lost their captain, Campbell Iredell, who was killed in the attack. The Federals retreated through the town of Gettysburg and took up positions on Cemetery Heights.

Maj. John T. Jones of the Twenty-Sixth North Carolina had this to say about what he saw:

> In our front was a wheat-field about a fourth of a mile wide; then came a branch, with thick underbrush and briars skirting the banks. Beyond this again was an open field, with the exception of a wooded hill directly in front of the Twenty-sixth Regiment, about covering its front. Skirmishes were being thrown out, we remained in line of battle until 2 p.m., when orders to advance were received. The brigade moved forward at beautiful style at quick time. . . . When nearing the branch . . . the enemy poured a galling fire into the left of the brigade from the opposite bank, where they had amassed in heavy force. . . . The Forty-seventh and Fifty-second, although exposed to a hot fire from artillery and infantry, lost but few in comparison to with the Eleventh and Twenty-sixth. On went the command across the branch and up

the opposite slope, driving the enemy at the point of the bayonet back upon their second line. . . . On this second line, the fighting was terrible—our men advancing, the enemy stubbornly resisting, until the two lines were pouring volleys into each other at a distance not greater than 20 paces. At last the enemy were compelled to give way. They again made a stand in the woods, and the third time they were driven from their position.[5]

With their portion of the fighting over for the day, the men dressed their lines and bivouacked right where they had started the charge earlier in the day. They had held their ground. The men told stories throughout the moonlit night, wondering what the next day would bring. There was a spirit of optimism, "intoxicated with victory" as Thorp put it, as the first day was no doubt a resounding Confederate success. Another man, William Blount said, "in this fight we showed the superiority of Southern Soldiers over Yankee hirelings."[6]

Gettysburg, Day 2

Pettigrew called up all his men, from those who had minor wounds all the way down to cooks. The Chicora Guards were held in reserve in the woods, behind the Confederate batteries facing Cemetery Hill and not engaged on the second day of the battle. While it was cooler, it was also frustrating and horrifying. Although it had proven worthy in battle, the unit had suffered great casualties.

They witnessed epic charges, bloodletting, and never-ending shelling all through the night, and the struggle at Little Round Top. A different mood settled over the camp that evening, in anticipation of the impending climax.

Gettysburg, Day 3

The next day would not be a spectator event. Wright and his fellow infantrymen were put in the front line of what would come to be known as Pickett's Charge. Thorp mentions that he never understood why history has regarded and attributed command to Pickett. In his eyewitness account, Captain Thorp said that Pickett supported Pettigrew, not the other way around, and that Pickett's distance to cover was much shorter than the field left to Pettigrew. "Just why [it was] called Pickett's instead of Pettigrew's Charge is not warranted by the facts," the captain wrote.[7] Long after the war there was controversy, as Pickett and his defenders tried to blame the North Carolina troops for the disaster, but records and eyewitness accounts show otherwise. Arguments have been made that because of the devastating losses on Day 1, the Tar Heels should not even have been involved in the attack.

At any rate, along with Twenty-Sixth North Carolina they entered the breech, an attack ordered by Lee on the Union center. The thousand-yard, quick-time march was straight into the line of fire, over open ground with numerous fence obstacles and offering little chance for the attackers to shoot. At 1 p.m. the artillery started, and it was so hot that several men fainted before the attack went off. Others said the battle seemed like an earthquake.

At 2 p.m. the order was given to advance, and the ridge in front of the Forty-Seventh gave an obstructed view. When Wright and his comrades passed the artillery, they could see the fences would be a problem, but they didn't hesitate; however, supporting troops on both sides were confused. The Federal artillery lit into the men of the Forty-Seventh when they were about a hundred yards into the advance and opened "great gaps" every "five or ten steps," but the Confederates managed to fill the holes quickly. When the men halted briefly at the Bliss farm, they were facing the Fourteenth Connecticut, which opened up on them with withering rifle fire from breech-loading rifles, or muskets that had been stockpiled and loaded, creating a rapid fire scenario. When there were no longer enough men to make up ranks, the men continued to advance in small groups. One witness said of the slaughter, "they seemed to sink into the earth under the tempest of the fire poured into them."[8]

Major Jones described the brigade's role in the Pickett-Petitgrew Charge:

> It was an open field in front, about three-quarters of a mile in in width. . . . When about half across the intervening space, the

enemy opened up on us a most destructive fire of grape and canister. When within about 250 or 300 yards of the stone wall behind
which the enemy was posted, we were met with a perfect hailstorm
of lead from their small arms. The brigade dashed on, and many
had reached the wall, when we received a deadly volley from the
left. The whole line on the left had given way, and we were being
rapidly flanked. With our thinned ranks and in such a position, it
would have been folly to stand, and against such odds. We therefore fell back to our original position in rear of the batteries.[9]

Groups ground to a halt while officers tried to figure out what to
do. Bullets were thick and buzzed like angry bees protecting a hive,
everywhere at once. The heat in the open field was nearly unbear-
able, before the maw of war enveloped it, and the intensity and chaos
only made it worse. Death hovered around and above every man it
had not already touched. Pettigrew was hit, as the men of the Forty-
Seventh and Twenty-Sixth made their way closer to the infamous
stone wall. The Twenty-Sixth advanced the farthest, echoing their
legacy years later with "First at Bethel, Farthest at Gettysburg, Last
at Appomattox." Colonel Graves and 150 of the remaining men in
the Forty-Seventh, including Wright, were captured, as many men
were trapped on the battlefield and cut off from their lines after the
most heated action subsided, not attempting to withdraw, as many
who did were cut down.

Before the rebels could be sent to the rear to be transported to
POW camps, however, Wright and several others took advantage of
the disorder and shifting lines and managed to escape from their
Union captors and made it back to their companies. This perhaps hinted for the first time at Wright's uncanny ability to survive. Colonel Faribault was wounded; Lieutenant Colonel Graves
was wounded and captured and later died in a prison camp; Maj.
Archibald Crudup was also wounded and captured. The rebels suffered over a 50 percent casualty rate, and Pettigrew's losses alone
numbered over two thousand. Wright managed to escape unscathed.

Several of Wright's friends were killed that afternoon. Richard
Dozier "died gallantly charging." Others cut down from Company

A were Williamson Abernathy, Jonathan Cockrell, Eli Joyner, Gilbert Lewis, Samuel Sellers, Marcus T. S. Strickland, and Emerson Puckett. Wounded were Lt. B. Dunn, Sgts. J. J. Barnhill, G. P. Westry, and Cone, as well as Frank Edwards, Martin Green, Lovett Boykin, Kinchen Joyner, Stephen Lamm, William Lamm, Gilliam Lewis, James Perry, Seymour Warren, and William Riley. Left on the field within Union picket lines were Sgt. J. J. Partin, Abijah Baines, Josiah Bissett, Neverson Cone, A. J. Henderson, J. B. O'Neill, J. A. Berry, B. J. Strickland, T. L. Strickland, and Wren Tisdale. There were thirteen thousand Confederates who were repelled on the mile-long battlefield. When it was over, the carnage had taken just one hour. Julius Rowan Rogers said, "The 47th acted bravely, cooly, and none faltered. All did their duty and acted the part of brave soldiers."[10] In all, 21 men from the regiment were killed and 140 wounded.

Sgt. A. H. Harris of Company C of the Forty-Seventh wrote a letter to the *Daily Progress*, which he dispatched from Winchester, Virginia, five days after the battle ended. It was printed on July 14 and read in part:

> I arrived yesterday from Gettysburg, Pa., the scene of the severest battle of the war, The fight commenced on the 1st, and lasted four days. Our Brigade (Pettigrews's) suffered severely on the first days' fight, in driving back a vastly superior force of the enemy supported by a strong battery. The 26th and 11th were literally cut to pieces. I remained unhurt until the third day's fight, when Heath's Division was ordered to charge the heights around Gettysburg. We moved forward under a most galling fire, and were twice repulsed. In the charge I was wounded through the leg, and had my shoulder very badly bruised. My rifle was shot to pieces in my hands. On Saturday evening, I was sent to Winchester with the other wounded, there being some two or three hundred wagon loads. . . . My company is completely annihilated. We have not half a dozen men, who went into the fight but were either killed or wounded. . . . Our loss has been tremendous, rumor says 20,000, and I do not think that an extravagant estimate.

The Forty-Seventh lost its battle flag on the third day, as did the Twenty-Sixth and the Fifty-Second. At the end of the day, men trickled back into camp, separated during the confusion, and fog of war, and the unending pounding of the earth. Some were wounded, some were not, and almost all were in a state of shock. The neutral ground between the armies was covered in bodies of the dead, and there were the unrelenting cries of the wounded and dying that echoed all night long. It was the sound of the Confederacy dying.

News reports in North Carolina must have caused tremendous worry among the home folks, particularly those in Nashville. The *Weekly Raleigh Register* reported in its July 15 edition:

> The news which we give to-day from the ensanguined field of Gettysburg will fall heavily on the ear and hearts of many persons in this State. The brigade of General Pettigrew suffered awfully in this battle—bloodiest of the war—and, as far as we can learn, the 26th and 47th Regiments were the most terribly cut up. Such a number of casualties among officers is unprecedented in the history of this war. . . . Many others in the this regiment . . . have not been heard from, and anxiety for their fate now, when there is an interruption of telegraphic communication, is most painful and trying.[11]

Thorp later wrote that the regiment returned "a skeleton of its former self . . . began business (on July 4) without a field officer." He added that the number of dead left in the field supply proof that "perhaps this assault was a Confederate mistake." The stakes had been high, with Harrisburg, Baltimore, and Washington DC, all at risk had things gone differently. Pettigrew gathered the men on July 4 and told them if they had succeeded, they would have been on the march to the Capitol and perhaps awaiting word of peace negotiations. Newspapers in Richmond immediately started blaming Pettigrew and defending native Virginian Pickett, although some think that there was confusion between Pettigrew's brigade and Heth's division. Newspapers in North Carolina rose to Pettigrew's defense, but the inaccuracies and debate would outlive almost all of the participants, well into the twentieth century. Virginia periodicals blamed Pettigrew and defended Pickett, and North Carolina writers took the opposite tact.[12]

Thorp believed that neither side realized the "bigness" in the immediate aftermath, and that is why the Union did not pursue Lee's decimated army and perhaps end the war then and there. Desertion rates increased heavily. Newspaper publisher Holden of the *North Carolina Standard*, an anti-secession, antiwar activist from the beginning, printed that the war was a mistake and called for a peace settlement. It was certainly the death knell of the CSA, the beginning of the end that would unfortunately not come quickly or cheaply or without additional enormous suffering.

Retreat

After speaking to the men, Pettigrew commanded the division as it started its retreat on July 4 in a heavy rain and retrieved the wounded from the battlefield. The brigade reached Hagerstown on July 7, and the Forty-Seventh was part of the rear guard covering as Lee moved his army across the flooded Potomac River on pontoon bridges at Falling Waters, Maryland. Most of the army crossed on July 13.

On the morning of July 14 the North Carolinians found themselves as the last units on the wrong side of river, with the Union army pushing closer and closer, skirmishing heavily. The men had moved all night through mud and rain and were exhausted. It would prove to be a fateful day, and some reports differ with Thorp's accounting. The captain wrote that a "drunken squad" of Union cavalry attacked the Forty-Seventh while they were resting, before the Confederates beat them back. In the furious exchange of fire and line breaks, the cavalry managed to cut off a number of Confederates from the bridge. Pettigrew's brigade suffered 56 percent casualties, and Pettigrew himself was mortally wounded. An element of Union cavalry attacked the camp and was at first mistaken for Confederates. One Union soldier shot several rebels with his Colt Revolver, and Pettigrew pulled his pistol to stop the man; it misfired. The cavalryman then shot the general in the stomach. Enraged Confederates chased the assailant to a nearby barn and beat him to death with a rock. Surgeons tried to get Pettigrew to allow himself to be captured so he could get proper treatment, but he refused and died three days later.[13]

The general's death left Maj. John T. Jones of the Twenty-Sixth as the only remaining field officer, and he barely escaped, mentioning in his notes, "We crossed the pontoons . . . just as the bridge was being cut loose."[14]

Bristoe Station

The brigade marched on for rest and refit at Orange Courthouse in Virginia. Brig. Gen. William Kirkland, promoted just weeks before from colonel, took over the brigade in September. Several wounded members of Company A returned along with Wright and others who had escaped or been separated, and new recruits arrived as replacements. By October the Army of Northern Virginia had taken up a defense near the Rapidan River, while Federal forces were aligned nearby on the Rappahannock River. Lee was trying to turn Meade's right flank and advance on Washington DC. On October 9 they marched toward Culpepper. Both armies were still weary from Gettysburg and, with winter coming, were maneuvering for position to launch spring campaigns. The Union Army sent reinforcements across the Blue Ridge to Chattanooga, and General Lee learned that he was now facing a less imposing force. He attacked General Meade's force across the Rapidan, pushing them back toward Centreville and Bristoe Station. General Heth's division was ordered by Gen. A. P. Hill, who did not realize he was greatly outnumbered, to engage the Union force there. Cooke's brigade retired; then Kirkland overtook Gen. Gouverneur K. Warren, who had distinguished himself at Gettysburg at Little Round Top and was in charge of a corps of Meade's army. Kirkland attacked without reinforcements, directly into entrenched Union positions, with both flanks exposed. The Battle of Bristoe Station ensued.

The battle opened in the early afternoon of October 14. An early shell burst took out fifteen men of the Forty-Seventh. A group of about forty skirmishers, including Wright, refused to rejoin the battle lines when they starting overlapping. These men did not run, but they refused to be part of yet another suicide charge that claimed so many of their friends at Gettysburg. The scene was familiar and seemed like Cemetery Ridge all over again. This time the men adjusted and formed their own plan of attack. The group crossed in front of the brigade and surged around the Eighty-Second New York. The Eleventh followed, and then part of the Fifty-Second did too. They managed to fire into the flank and rear of the New Yorkers, but the success was temporary. The Federals loaded canister rounds, and after the bloody mess in Pennsylvania, many men were "unwilling to expose themselves"; they retired or took cover in the barns of the locals, as well as some huts in an overrun Federal camp. Heth was captured, and Kirkland was wounded. Soon the attack stalled and was doomed. The Forty-Seventh had marched fourteen miles that day and had not eaten, and the men were flanked and ordered to retreat. To do so they would have to cross open ground under heavy fire, which would have been suicidal—this had been proven several times. With Pickett's disaster fresh on their minds, many men refused to move and held their ground. There was chaos.

"Nearly every man of strong voice was bawling out something of which I could distinguish the following: 'cease fire,' 'lie down,' 'don't shoot, you are shooting our own men,' 'charge,' 'fall back,' and the like, so that it was impossible to recognize the voice of our commander unless very near him," said Thomas Bailey, a private in the Forty-Seventh. Two brigades were slaughtered. It was a "great blunder on the part of A. P. Hill," Thorp wrote.[15] Lt. Sidney Bridgers was killed. Wright and several members of the Chicora Guards were soon surrounded and forced to surrender. This time there would be no escape.

Confederate losses at Bristoe Station were over 1,300, with a lot of men missing. The Forty-Seventh had 5 killed and 37 wounded. Bristoe Station was another disaster, and Gen. A. P. Hill took the blame from Lee, the men, and the newspapers. It is not known whether Sally Batchelor heard about the list of casualties from Company A reported in the October 28, 1863, edition of the *Daily Progress* in North Carolina. It listed Lt. G. W. Westray as severely wounded in the thigh, and Lt. S. H. Bridgers as mortally wounded. Color Cpl.

William Chamblee was wounded severely in the hip; Pvts. A. P. Arnswell and William F. Edwards were wounded in the shoulder and foot, respectively; also shot were Pvts. Abuja Griffin (leg), William G. Murray (side and arm), and William Tolbert (head). On the missing list were Sgt. Charles Braswell, Cpl. J. C. Eatman, Pvts. Irvin C. Eatman, Lovett Boykin, Calvin Burnett, Jesse Davis, John Finch, D. A. Glover, A. J. Glover, T. Glover, Yancey Glover, J. Hogwood, Isham Hagwood, Bartley Jones, Joseph Manning, William R. Morgan, Elijah W. Patterson, Sidney S. Patterson, William Taylor, John Turner, John Ward, B. B. Batchelor (or Richard B.), and W. S. Batchelor. Others wounded from Company A were Sgt. John J. Barnhill, Manoah Bissett, and Kinchen Joyner.

Thorp recorded in his notes: "And may be . . . that a kind Providence had heard prayers for the Union that has ascended both sides, though uttered not so loud from the South, and in answer, just wrote down in the book of Fate: 'Gettysburg 3 July, 1863, the beginning of the end.'"[16]

For Wright and several of his fellow soldiers, the war was getting ready to take some crazy turns. For the remaining men, the rest of the war would be a series of privations and frustrations.

8

The Home Front

You people of the south don't know what you are doing.
This country will be drenched in blood, and God only knows
how it will end. It is all folly, madness. . . . You mistake, too, the
people of the North. . . . They are not going to let this country
be destroyed without a mighty effort to save it. . . . You are bound
to fail. Only in your spirit and determination are you prepared
for war. In all else you are totally unprepared, with a bad cause
to start with. At first you will make headway, but as your limited
resources begin to fail, shut out from the markets of Europe as
you will be, your cause will begin to wane. If your people will but
stop and think, they must see in the end that you will surely fail.

—WILLIAM T. SHERMAN at the Louisiana State Seminary,
December 1860

There wasn't a lot of action in Nash County during the war, but
not long after the Confederate Army's crushing defeat at Gettysburg, the Union Army moved across eastern North Carolina and
did some damage back in Rocky Mount, not far from Wright's
home outside Nashville.

Technically Rocky Mount Mills *was* Rocky Mount prior to the
war. There wasn't an officially incorporated town of Rocky Mount
until after the war, and the two entities remained separate until the
early twentieth century.

On a striking plot of land, hilly and rocky and ideal to harness waterpower, Joel Battle and two partners started in 1818 what was one of the first two cotton mills in the state, built by slave labor and located on twenty acres at the Falls of the Tar River. The mill was "of rock-granite-with which the spot so abounds, and three stories high with a basement" and powered by a large dam, which also powered a gristmill.[1] Some reports state the original building had six stories. Battle, who was educated at and later had a son who served as president of the University of North Carolina, died in 1829, and his family continued to operate the company. Slaves worked the operation until 1852, when the Battles went to hired labor, mostly women and girls. It was one of the biggest industrial locations in North Carolina, employing around fifty workers, who by the 1860s were making about $2.50 a week.[2] Many of the workers lived in houses nearby that were part of the property and formed what became known as the mill village. Rocky Mount had free blacks and black landowners. As a huge supplier of cotton and other stores for the Confederacy, it was a prime target when the Union started its North Carolina campaign.

The Federal plan was to take Roanoke Island, then move to Goldsboro, and after that Raleigh. Gen. Ambrose Burnside had taken New Bern, but he was called to Richmond to support Gen. George McClellan. Operating out of New Bern, Gen. John G. Foster sent Brig. Gen. Edward Potter on a raid that targeted the nearby towns of Greenville, Tarboro, and Rocky Mount. The Wilmington and Weldon Railroad, which ran through Rocky Mount, was a key artery in keeping the Confederates supplied, in addition to the significance of Rocky Mount Mills to the war effort. On July 19 the force found strong entrenchments outside Greenville, but there were no troops manning them. The Federals destroyed $300,000 worth of property, robbed local citizens, got drunk, and burned the Tar River bridge. They then resumed the march to Tarboro, a smaller but significant town fewer than twenty miles to the northwest in Edgecombe County.

At Sparta ("Old Sparta," not to be confused with Sparta in western North Carolina), a community south of Tarboro on the route to Greenville, the group split into two elements, with Maj. Ferris

Jacobs of the Third New York Cavalry assigned to go on to Rocky
Mount with six companies to destroy the railroad bridge and whatever government property he could. The first group made it to Tarboro around 7 or 8 a.m. and found only light resistance from a few
scattered rebels, who fired shots and took off. The Federals found
an ironclad and two steamboats, which they destroyed along with
"some railroad cars, 100 bales of cotton, the quartermaster's sub-
sistence and ordnance stores."[3] Then, as if clocking out of work,
the men went to the town's hotel and ate a meal before burning
the Tar River bridge and returning to New Bern.

Rocky Mount proved to be a sweeter target than anticipated. The
Union forces again met little resistance and captured a train with
five officers and ten privates aboard. Just before daybreak, a Union
private took off after a departing locomotive, jumped aboard, placed
a gun to the head of the engineer, and ordered him to back the train
to the depot.[4] The engineer complied. Troops then destroyed and
burned the depot and telegraph offices, the railroad and telegraph
lines, a county bridge, and the railroad bridge, including all the tres-
tlework. They evacuated about 150 white females before setting the
main mill building on fire and then proceeded to wreck a government flour mill, a thousand barrels of flour, manufactured goods,
two thousand spindles, a large building used for spinning and weav-
ing, the gristmill, cotton gin, sawmill, machine shop, another shop
with munitions, storehouses, and other supplies and wagons along
with "immense quantities of hardtack." About eight hundred bales
of cotton were burned. One of Potter's men reported, "the destruction of property was large and complete."[5] In addition to the cotton's use in clothing, it was also used to make ammunition. Local
legend has it that the Battle home was spared because the mill's
superintendent was a Northerner and convinced a Union officer
who was a fellow Mason not to torch the home.[6] It was likely that
Sally Ann and her neighbors back in the Nashville area, barely ten
miles away, saw the fire and smoke and what had to be relentless
explosions. It must have seemed as if the war was not only close;
it was at the front door, with the army in retreat through Pennsylvania, Maryland, and Virginia.

The troops marched back to Tarboro with prisoners and burned five more wagons and more cotton before heading back to New Bern. When the Federal army reached Tarboro, it is said they were going to burn the home of Frederick Proctor. Proctor was absent, and his wife was sick in bed. The three young Proctor daughters begged the soldiers not to burn the house, cotton gin, and barns and finally struck a bargain when they offered to fill all the Yankee canteens with brandy.[7]

The Wilmington and Weldon Railroad kept a labor force on call for repairs and had the railroad bridge back in operation by August 1. The mills did not get rebuilt until after the war and then burned again in 1869, that time reportedly by a disgruntled worker.

Nearby Wilson was not threatened by the raiding party, but when word of the damage reached the town, the militia fled to the woods. Only the men defending the Confederate war hospital in town took up arms. On the return trip the Union was pursued around Old Sparta and harassed all the way back to New Bern. They returned from the mission with one hundred prisoners of war, three hundred horses and mules, and three hundred "contraband" (slaves). The killed, wounded, and missing numbered fewer than seventy-five.

The citizens of eastern North Carolina petitioned Governor Vance for help, but there wasn't much he could do, and another attack was launched shortly afterward on Weldon, a key railroad center in neighboring Halifax County.

United States Elections Held in Confederacy

As late as midway through the war, President Lincoln held out hope of peacefully luring back the reluctant Confederate state, North Carolina, into the Union through a loophole.

In late 1862 and early 1863, the Union held congressional elections in four districts in North Carolina, Virginia, Tennessee, and Louisiana. At least ten times in the U.S. Senate and thirty times in the House, men applied for admission to the bodies claiming to represent their states or districts in the Confederacy. Some were from districts that had repudiated secession, but others were simply looking for steady work and a paycheck.

As the Union seized control of large portions of eastern North Carolina, Lincoln appointed Edward Stanly as military governor of the state. Stanly's family was from New Bern, but he had moved to California in 1853 to practice law. In February 1862 he offered his services to Lincoln, suggesting he could help bring North Carolina back into the United States. Many Northern conservatives were pleased at first, because they wanted the Union restored, even with slavery intact. Lincoln stated during his preliminary talk about the Emancipation Proclamation that representation in Congress would be taken as proof of renewed allegiance, and that states or parts of states represented on January 1, 1863, would be exempt from the Proclamation. The large contingent of pro-Union men in North Carolina seized on this potential loophole as perhaps enough to end the war in the Tar Heel state. Lincoln thought North Carolina was ripe to be turned. "It is my sincere wish that North Carolina may again govern herself conformably to the Constitution of the United States," he said.[8]

The pro-Union *New Bern Progress* newspaper supported the election and wrote that the war was "not one of subjugation and destruction, but of deliverance and restoration." There were problems with the plan from the start, however. Stanly lost much of his abolitionist support when he refused to approve Negro schools in New Bern. Second, seven counties in the Second District were under control of the Confederacy, and the Union really only had the towns of New Bern, Washington, and Beaufort under control. Several men presented themselves as candidates, but in the end the race came down to Charles Henry Foster and Jennings Piggott. Foster had tried to claim a seat in Congress and was viewed as a crook by many, and Piggott had been in Washington and only came down as a move by Stanly and others to block Foster. Many resented Piggott since he'd left the area and was considered the "establishment" candidate, and many of the Unionists thought he was "secesh," or supportive of secession, and didn't trust him. Foster and Stanly did not like each other and took to the stump frequently—Foster's supporters were not just against slavery; they were against slaveowners and slaves and saw emancipation as the first step toward deportation. Many were members of "free labor associations."[9]

North Carolina had its election in the Second District on January 1, 1863. The election was authorized by Lincoln and was an attempt to restore North Carolina to the Union. There was clearly antagonism between "the better sort" and the nonslaveholders in the state, the latter of which were doing most of the suffering during the war.

All "loyal" free white men aged twenty-one or older who had lived in the county where they voted could vote, and no loyalty oath was required. Elections were to be held in other parts of the state where citizens wanted them. When the election finally came, only nineteen precincts in three counties—Carteret, Craven, and Hyde—were open. The magistrate in Washington refused to open the polls, and polls couldn't be opened in Pitt, Lenoir, Greene, Wayne, Onslow, Edgecombe, and Jones Counties. Only 864 total votes were cast, and Piggott won with 595 votes. The House Committee on Elections met in February 1862 and ruled against Piggott, claiming he was not an inhabitant. Stanly felt that the Emancipation Proclamation had eliminated any chance of North Carolina peaceably returning to the Union, and he resigned and returned to California. Lincoln abandoned hope as well and did not appoint a replacement. It was a long shot, but North Carolina had missed a chance to change its course.

When the rumblings began that the Confederacy was going to begin conscription, or a draft, as it had become obvious that despite early enthusiasm, the rebels were outnumbered greatly in most every theater of action. There was staunch opposition to this among the people, especially in North Carolina. This was viewed by many as a central government overreach, an irony not lost on those whose cause was dependent on individual rights. The CSA would repeatedly make the mistake of intrusions into citizens' lives to the point that internal conflicts may have been as responsible for the South losing the war as battlefield losses.

At home, in addition to the Conscription Act of 1862, a "tithe" of 10 percent of all produce raised by farmers had to be handed over to the Confederacy as a tax and to ease already stressed supply lines.

Specific committees were appointed that could confiscate livestock, provisions, wagons, and even slaves in the name of the war effort.

In 1862 Vance was the nominee for governor by the Conservative Party and ran against railroad executive and Confederate Party nominee William Johnston. Johnston and others tried to paint Vance as a Union sympathizer or the "Yankee candidate." Vance and his supporters blamed the Confederate government for inflation, battle losses, the draft, and the lack of support for the families of soldiers off fighting the war. Inflation was a huge problem, putting food out of the reach of many families left behind by a labor force that had gone off to war. Vance won overwhelmingly with 73 percent of the vote, but he barely carried Nash County 317–282 and was soundly trounced in Edgecombe 508–113.[10]

By the time Rocky Mills was burned, there was strong opposition and protest to the draft all across the state, as well as the South in general. By the end of 1863 the coastal plain of North Carolina was almost completely occupied by Union forces, and the mountains were full of deserters and rogue units, as well as roving bands of vigilante "home guards," all contributing to inner turmoil that helped unravel the CSA internally, mirroring what was happening on the battlefield. General Lee complained to Secretary of War James Seddon of "frequent desertions from North Carolina regiments."[11]

W. W. Holden, the editor of one of the state's leading newspapers, the *North Carolina Standard*, a vocal opponent of secession and war, began calling for peace at any price after Gettysburg. Holden, a key operative in the Democratic Party before the war, had aspirations on the governor's office. He'd helped Vance get elected to the post, endorsing him in 1862, but his newspaper stances had put him on the outs with the Democrats. The state was torn, and this is no better illustrated than by the violence taken out that summer on two Raleigh papers. A Georgia regiment passing through the state capital destroyed Holden's newspaper office, and immediately afterward Holden's supporters trashed the *State Journal*, a pro-war newspaper, in retaliation.

Make no mistake though, Holden and his Peace Party of 1863 were not abolitionists. In a July 1863 column in the *North Caro-*

lina Standard, he wrote: "We favor peace because we believe that peace now would save slavery, while we very much fear that a prolongation of the war will obliterate the last vestige of it." The party won six of the ten seats in the Confederate Congress that year.[12]

Peace meetings were held throughout the state, and there was talk of seceding from the Confederacy—with ideas to rejoin the Union. There were also those who were for remaining out of alignment with either warring faction. There were at least a hundred meetings in at least forty counties after the defeats at Vicksburg and Gettysburg, and there was legitimate concern in both Raleigh and Richmond that North Carolina was on the verge of leaving the CSA. The Union Army did not help itself garner more support, however, as looting was rampant across occupied areas. There is a belief that North Carolina's internal conflict was one reason General Sherman was restrained when he later tore through the state.

Holden's push for peace split him with the Peace Party and with Vance, who at times battled the Confederacy himself. Vance clashed with Jefferson Davis over the draft, the use of Virginia officers in North Carolina, and discrimination in the appointment and promotion of North Carolina officers. However, Vance could see no sense in seceding from the secessionist states, instead parroting, "Fight the Yankees and fuss with the Confederacy," all throughout his 1864 campaign.[13] Holden opposed him that year as the nominee from the Peace Party. Vance won easily.

Although North Carolina was one of the leading dissenters, the Confederacy had problems all over. Davis was constantly at odds with the House and Senate, and even with his own cabinet. Vice President Stephens refused to live in the same state as Davis. None of the leaders wanted to bend. Some states wanted to operate as separate, sovereign nations. Arkansas governor Henry Rector wanted his state to leave the Confederacy in the summer of 1862, and such sentiment grew to the point that in early 1863 an amendment was proposed in Congress to let Confederate states secede. In great irony, the measure was dropped.[14]

Times were tough at home as Confederate money became more devalued and inflation skyrocketed. Bacon went from 33 cents a pound to $7.50. A bushel of wheat that had been $3 sold for $50, and coffee was upward of $100 a pound. There was high demand and low supply for food, and many women struggled to support families without much help. Sally Ann and women like her had to do all of the men's jobs related to the farm in addition to their regular chores and running the household. Facing life-threatening shortages, groups of women banded together across the state to raid supply stores and shops, mostly targeting those owned by speculators. The most famous of these "Bread Riots" occurred near Charlotte in Salisbury in 1863, and these uprisings continued well into 1865.[15] Some women, missing loved ones and sometimes not hearing from their menfolk for months, resorted to visiting seers such as "Aunt Hester" Brantley in Nash County, who lived in A. H. Arrington's part of the county. For a chicken or a ham, Brantley could inform an anxious wife if she was or was about to be a widow, or if her man was safe from Yankee bullets.[16]

Shortly after Wright's capture, on November 1, 1863, the Forty-Seventh executed a deserter, with the entire brigade formed in ranks. This was the beginning of a harsh crackdown on desertions, and justice for this varied. Sometimes no punishment was issued at all, sometimes men were made into examples. For the troops, morale was down after the two major defeats at Gettysburg and Bristoe Station, and there was a lack of food, equipment, supplies, and even firewood. Often times men had been separated from family for long stretches without leave and had every intention of returning after they visited the home folks, especially if their units were operating near home and leaves weren't granted. Most of the men were far from home and took unauthorized leave to visit families, tend to sick relatives, or help with crops. Letters from home urged them to come home.[17] North Carolina had about twenty-three thousand deserters during the war, of which around eight thousand returned. The rate was in line with the rest of the Confederate states. The Confederate Army executed about two hundred men for desertion over the course of the war. Several hundred more were sentenced, but the penalties were overturned.

Draft evasions, peace movements, desertion, and even armed resistance threw whole regions of the state into near anarchy. This should not have been a surprise based on North Carolina's reluctance to join the Confederacy. After many of the military failures, some men simply refused to fight. There was a lot of resistance to the draft, and many men joined the Home Guard or militia. Some of these groups proved to be no more than vigilantes who rounded up deserters, or in some cases deserters formed themselves into rogue groups, with many operating in the mountains. Some terrorized citizens and operated as gangs.

The North Carolina Legislature created the Home Guard on July 7, 1863, just after the crushing defeat at Gettysburg. It was an emergency police force composed of all white men from ages eighteen to fifty who were exempted from regular service. The Home Guard outfits were either First, Second, or Third Class, depending on the physical condition of the men, and each county had at least one unit. Men could be called into service for three months at a time for public defense. North Carolina's Home Guard consisted of twelve thousand men and spent its time like the rest of those across the Confederacy—rounding up deserters, maintaining law and order, skirmishing with Union forces, and guarding prisoners of war. That same year the Confederacy put in place a progressive income tax and other taxes, much like the Union, to fund the war.[18]

It wasn't just the soldiers who tired of the war. Many came to oppose the CSA because of the sacrifices it demanded from the common poor people. In addition to the draft being considered a government overreach, there were crop impressments, suspension of some civil liberties, and exemptions from the service for plantation owners who had twenty or more slaves. Less than 30 percent of the population of North Carolina owned slaves, so economic disparity certainly divided the classes even more.

One Southern farmer from another state who went AWOL said he "did not propose to fight for the rich men while they were at home having a good time." The law was modified later and required slaveholders who were exempted to sell to the government goods at fixed prices; for example, they might be required to sell two hundred pounds of meat per year, a part of which was supposed to be distributed to the families of soldiers.[19]

Back on the Batchelor farm, Sally Ann and the children were having to make due the best they could. In addition to keeping the house, Sally Ann had to do all of Wright's work in the fields to keep everyone fed. The children fed the animals, milked the cows, and collected the eggs, among other chores usually reserved for older kids or adults. Her neighbors faced the same hardships, and they often pitched in to help each other.

In September 1862 the draft age was raised to forty-five, and by February 1864 the draft eligible ages were changed to include men seventeen to fifty. North Carolina's military age population was 115,369, but 125,000 men served during the war. Governor Vance was adamantly opposed to the draft, as was the governor of Georgia. To them this was no better than the federal government's interference into states' rights. In early 1864 the Substitution Act was repealed. This controversial law allowed a draftee to avoid service by hiring a substitute who had been exempted by age or profession. Foreign nationals could also be hired. Both sides used the practice. Typically a fee was paid to the government and another fee to the substitute; there were even brokers who would find a substitute. Fees for Confederate substitutes are reported to have reached $3,000, an amount only the wealthy could afford. After the end of the Substitution Act, the Confederate Congress made men who had hired substitutes eligible for service and kept the substitute in the service as well. Even though a North Carolina Supreme Court justice ruled this was unconstitutional, the full court overruled him. Wright's brother Vincent served as a substitute and died early in the war.

There were exemptions for certain occupations. Railroad workers, river workers, civil officers, telegraph operators, miners, druggists, and teachers were not drafted. Many citizens were able to avoid the draft by having their names added as civil servants or to militia rosters, and 92 percent of all the exemptions in the Confederacy came from North Carolina and Georgia.

Many who served only did so under fear of retribution for not reporting for duty. War opponents, including Quakers, were often beaten, maimed, or otherwise abused and assaulted for not joining the Confederate Army or for speaking against the war.

Despite his complicity in aiding draft dodgers, and his early opposition to secession, Vance came out with strong words for deserters in May 1863 with a proclamation offering these words, among others, for deserters:

> Indictment and punishment in the civil courts of the Confederacy, as well as to the everlasting contempt and detestation of all good and honorable men. Certainly no crime could be greater, no cowardice more abject, no treason more base, than for a citizen of the State, enjoying its privileges and protection without sharing its dangers, to persuade those who have had the courage to go forth in defence of their country, vilely to desert the colors which they have sworn to uphold, when a miserable death or a vile and ignominious existence must be the inevitable consequences. No plea can excuse it.

He also shamed those who sheltered or abetted the men who left their posts. Threats were made to shoot both deserters and those who harbored them, even fathers and brothers, although men who returned to duty voluntarily would be spared the firing squad or noose. Despite all this, an underground railroad for those who managed to escape service in the CSA Army or those who wanted to serve in the Union Army was very active during the war. North Carolina had two mounted infantry, five regular infantry, and one artillery unit in Union service during the war. While no Nash County white men are recorded to have signed up for Union service at the beginning of the war, the county did have twenty-two former slaves or freedmen who served in the Colored Troops.[20]

Secretary of the Treasury Christopher Memminger recommended that the South resort to accepting counterfeit money. The bills were exchanged for a 6 percent call certificate, then stamped and validated, and reissued. Supplies requisitioned by the government and the army exceeded the amount of money in circulation by as much as 50 percent. Adding to the problem was the terrible incompetence of the Confederate government. Many of the crops and impressed goods ended up rotting in storage, never benefiting the troops in the field they were intended to reach, and continuing hard times on the citizens. It is fair to say that impressment officers were as despised as any potential Yankee invader. Price ceilings were set but not adhered to. For example, in 1863 corn was capped at $3 a bushel, but the actual price in 1864 was $19.25; bacon was 85 cents a pound and sold for $5.75; beef was 20 cents a pound and sold for $5.75; and a fifty-pound bag of salt with a ceiling of $8 was going for $63.[21] By 1864 a $100 North Carolina Bond was worth $7.40, and a Confederate one of the same face value was worth $4. As the war was winding down, things got worse as a bushel of salt rocketed to $173, rice $200, flour $529, corn meal $55, and a dozen eggs went for $8.25.[22]

Only a handful of North Carolinians made the rank of general in the Confederate Army: Braxton Bragg, D. H. Hill, Stephen Dodson Ramseur, Robert F. Hoke, James Pettigrew, L. O. B. Branch, and Bryan Grimes, in addition to two from the Nash–Edgecombe–Rocky Mount area. William Gaston Lewis from Rocky Mount served from Bethel until he was later captured at Farmville, Virginia, days before the surrender, and William Dorsey Pender of Edgecombe, who died a few weeks after being severely wounded at Gettysburg.

Officers in units were elected to their positions, and often the criteria was education, wealth, or leadership ability, which meant many field officers were unqualified or outright incompetent. There was a lot of sentiment that North Carolina men didn't get many appointments because of the question of the state's loyalty, even though the state supplied the most men of any during the war. When Capt. James Kincaid of the Fifty-Second was captured and had a conversation with Cpl. Alexander McNeil of the Fourteenth Connecticut, he said the "South had been rough and harsh with North Carolina troops since the war started, because North Carolina didn't secede quite soon enough to suit other states, and that South Carolina ought to be sunk."[23]

The wave of discontent had local political casualties as well. A. H. Arrington lost his bid for reelection in 1863 and did not even manage to carry his home county of Nash in the Fifth District, which also included Wake, Orange, Granville, Warren, and Franklin Counties.

There was a great deal of dissatisfaction with the Jefferson Davis administration. There were many citizens who wanted to return to the United States and/or secede from the CSA. Ironically Vance argued that the acceptance of the Confederate Constitution banned it, and that secession would cause the CSA to declare war on North Carolina and plunge it "in a deeper and bloodier war."[24] In the end the state officially stayed loyal to the Confederacy. As long as the general population felt they were fighting off a Federal invasion and battling an oppressive Federal government, people supported the war.[25] Many felt it was no different from the American Revolution break from Britain. Fighting for slavery, from the mostly non-slaveholding citizenry and military, was another story, although the Emancipation Proclamation issued in January 1863 made it clear that the war was about more than preserving the Union. It also served to hold off the Europeans who were poised to aid the South but didn't want to appear to support slavery.

Nash County supplied around 1,000 men to the Confederate cause. The state's troops and Home Guard numbered nearly 134,000, and the state "also furnished a large number of negroes from time to time to work on fortifications."[26] As the war continued to drag on, especially after Gettysburg, internal divisions in the South proved to be a large part of its undoing. Even Vance had to admit by 1864 that the situation in North Carolina was this: "The great popular heart is not now and never has been in this war. It was a revolution of the politicians, not the people."[27]

9

POW Life Leads to Being Galvanized ... and a Great Escape

Galvanized: a term used to describe metal that has been coated
to protect it from corrosion. The surface color of the metal
changes in this process, but when the coating is scraped
away, the original, true color is still there.

Wright and the others captured from his company were immediately sent to Old Capitol Prison in Washington DC on October 15, 1863. The men from Company A were William Boon, Lovett Boykin, Charles Braswell, Lemuel Braswell, Calvin Burnett, Jesse Davis, Irvin Eatman, John Finch, Vine Glover, Yancey Glover, Isham Hagwood, Bartley Jones, Joseph Manning, William Morgan, Elijah Patterson, Sidney Patterson, William Taylor, John Turner, and John A. Ward. Twelve days later they were transferred to one of the Civil War's most notorious prisoner-of-war camps, Point Lookout, also known as Camp Hoffman, in Maryland. At least fifty-two other men from the unit would spend time at Point Lookout over the course of the war. Seven of them died there.

Point Lookout is at the extreme southern tip of Maryland in St. Mary's County, where the Potomac River meets the Chesapeake Bay. The river was fifteen miles wide, and the bay a hundred miles wide at the time. It was a low, sandy pit, and marshy, about five feet below sea level, open and exposed—blazing hot in the summer and freezing cold in the winter. A military hospital was constructed in 1862, and additional buildings were added to house Southern sympathizers and political prisoners. The camp was made ready for Confederate prisoners after the Battle of Gettysburg. There were even several women among the prisoners, mostly those captured from blockade runners. Later, additional buildings were added in a spoke arrangement, as was a hospital for the prisoners. The camp covered about forty acres total, within two enclosures. The walls were fourteen feet high in some places.

Point Lookout was surrounded on three sides by water, and cannon pointed from the other side of the river from Fort Lincoln and Union gunboats. Armed guards had orders to shoot anyone who came within ten to twenty-five feet (accounts vary among sources and former prisoners) of a ditch near the wall—known as the Dead Line.

Conditions at the prison were among the worst in the war. It was built to house ten thousand prisoners, but after exchanges were discontinued, the ranks swelled to around twice that many. At any one time, there were twelve thousand to twenty thousand prisoners confined.[1] Union inspectors recommended wooden barracks be built, but Secretary of War Edwin Stanton refused to authorize them, requiring prisoners to sleep in tents but supplying an inadequate number. Point Lookout was the only Union prison without barracks, the hardline taken in response to reported conditions at the prisons in Andersonville, Georgia, and Salisbury, North Carolina— infamous, inhumane horror camps in the South. At one point a small tent housed seven to sixteen Confederates. The tents were about seven square feet, with no floor, no straw, and no extra blanket to put on the ground. Men would often pair up, putting one blanket as the floor and sleeping under the other. Union general Ethan Allen Hitchcock of the War Department defended this by saying, "As every soldier knows . . . [tents] are easily made comfortable, and are always thankfully received by the trooper in the field."[2]

It is almost impossible to determine exact rations and routines because accounts of POWs are often exaggerated and were in most cases written from memory, decades after confinement. But enough accounts are consistent to give some idea of life at Point Lookout. Roll call was at 6 a.m. The men lined up for a pint of coffee, a partial loaf of bread, and sometimes a piece of raw fish; there was seldom wood for cooking, so many men ate the fish raw. Between midmorning and early afternoon the same cup was filled with pea or bean soup, a piece of bread, and occasionally a small piece of corned beef or salt pork, around four ounces. Sometimes, there might be a spoon or "gill" (quarter of a pint) of molasses. Bread and sometimes crackers or about three ounces of hardtack were issued to sergeants to distribute as they saw fit. Sometimes there might be tea or a couple of gills of rice. This completed the day's rations. Some Confederates later said the sparse rations were no less than what they'd had in the army. Some men washed the clothes of others for extra rations, and thefts of rations, and the ensuing fights, were regular events. With rations and portions being small, men got creative. A man who reported as sick could get his rations brought to his tent. Many men did this, and then made their way to the chow line, in a ruse known as "flanking."[3] To keep from starving, prisoners often ate rats. Being on a work detail meant extra rations, or a plug of tobacco, or sometimes firewood. A black market developed, and gambling (Keno) was popular. No one wanted Confederate money or "shinplaster," as it was called, and it traded for about five cents on the dollar.

Religious services were held on weekdays and on Sundays; ministers from Baltimore and Washington DC came in rotation. Thousands were baptized.

The POW hospital was composed of eighteen tents. There were six wells with pumps, but only one was suitable for drinking. If water was left out overnight, it turned green because of the high copper content. Disease was rampant, and scurvy, malnutrition, lice, diarrhea, malaria, typhoid fever, and smallpox were common. Union inspection reports called Point Lookout "filthy." Health standards in the nineteenth century were poor in general compared to today, but sanitation in prison camps was atrocious. If disease didn't kill, the elements sometimes would, and some men froze to death. Reports were made ordering camp officials not to let the prisoners go naked. In November 1863 every transfer of POWs from Fort Delaware to Point Lookout had smallpox. Every day twenty to thirty men were sent to the hospital, and of the fifty-two thousand prisoners who passed through the gates, more than four thousand died. The mortality rate was higher than Andersonville.[4] The sick were filthy, often went without medical care, and sometimes were on half rations.[5] The Sanitary Commission reported deaths of 30 percent but said that POWs were treated the same as soldiers in the Union Army.[6] The tents were set up only a few inches above high tide, and there was typically not enough wood for more than two hours out of twenty-four in the winter. Reports of poor treatment and rations were denied by the commander, Gen. William H. Hoffman. Health advocate Dorothea Dix, "convinced that the North maintained exemplary prisons while the South committed unspeakable atrocities," found "there was nothing which could be objected to, and so much to commend that I sum up all in saying that there is no [change] called for," although a year later a new hospital was built.[7]

In October 1863, when Wright Batchelor arrived, an inspection revealed that many of the Confederates stated they did not wish to be exchanged, and some even mentioned an interest in joining the Union Navy. By November some took an oath of loyalty and officially switched sides. It was a ticket out of the camp, and a chance at surviving the war. These newly minted soldiers were mustered and drilled near the point, and the POWs who remained in camp started referring to them as "galvanized rebels." This was a derogatory term among Confederates, as was the term "white-washed Rebs." During the Civil War, the term "Galvanized Yankees" came into the vernacular to describe Confederates who joined the Union Army after being taken as prisoners of war (some Union soldiers joined the CSA Army during the war but in far fewer numbers). While totals are hard to determine, it is believed as many as eight thousand Southerners changed sides during the conflict. Some may have had a change of heart, some may have been looking for an easier opportunity to escape, but for many the odds of survival seemed better carrying a rifle than overcoming prison camp conditions. Records show that between the two sides, fifty-six thousand men died as prisoners of war.

As conditions worsened, taking the oath of allegiance and joining the Union Army not only became appealing, it became a real consideration for those who wanted to make it back home alive. On December 17 inspectors ordered that conditions be improved at the camp, as water contamination had become a serious problem. There was a shortage of clothing, and many men were heading into the winter without shoes or pants. Many county locals were Southern sympathizers and tried to get food and clothing to the prisoners. Aid to the prisoners was often denied in retribution to reports about what was being done to Union prisoners in Southern prison camps.

Lee planned a couple of attempts to liberate the camp, sending Gen. Jubal Early to the Washington DC area in the winter. There was another push in the summer of 1864, but neither resulted in a serious action.

There weren't a lot of escape attempts due to the nature of the camp's geography and the orders to shoot those who tried. The guards were made up of one regiment of New Hampshire volunteers and two regiments of Negro troops, from North and South Carolina, most of them escaped or freed slaves. As expected, there was much animosity between them and many of the prisoners. No doubt armed black men having authority over white men was a problem for a great many of the Southerners, and the chance to torment proxies of their former masters was most certainly an unavoidable temptation for the guards. There were rumors of guards randomly firing into groups of prisoners, and of freed slaves who served as guards earning promotions for killing Confederates. One account said that Union general Benjamin Butler rode his horse into groups of prisoners for sport, striking down several of them. One Confederate later said, "Murder was not only sampled, but opportunities sought for its commission by the guards, who were known to have been offered by the Officer of the Day as much as $10 and $15 apiece for every prisoner they could shoot in the discharge of their duty." Accounts after the war, particularly those in issues of *Confederate Veteran*, offered many anecdotes of mistreatment. One veteran, Sgt. N. F. Harman of Georgia, said that guards patrolled in pairs down each street in the camp, which was known as a division. Prisoners had to be in their tents after taps, with no talking. These patrols would reportedly call men out of the tents and chase them down the streets to exhaustion. Guards often asked prisoners for their addresses, so they could "write to the prisoner's sister." One report offered that guards claimed the men in one tent were talking and fired into it, killing them all. Commanders of the camp shrugged their shoulders and carried on.

The winter of 1863 and 1864 was a tough one. Jesse Davis died in October. Jackson Bissette and Lemuel Braswell died in December. William Bass died in March, and before the war was over Robert Abernathy, Calvin Burnett, and Whitley Perry also passed. Wright wouldn't be there to see the last of his friends die.

By February Wright had reached his limit. Death, sickness, and hardship surrounded him. There was no point living that way when there was a ticket out. On February 24, 1864, he took the Oath of Allegiance to the Union and joined the army. He wasn't alone; around 12 percent of the POWs did the same, and 40 percent of them were North Carolinians, reluctant secessionists who had little to gain regardless of which side won the war. They included Boon and Caswell Matthews, who'd been captured at Falling Waters, Company C's Sergeant Braswell, and Company D's Morgan. The oath they took read this way:

> I do solemnly swear in the presence of Almighty God, that I will Henceforth faithfully support, protect, and defend the Constitution of the United States and the Union of States there-under, and that I will, in like manner, abide by and faithfully support all acts of Congress passed during the existing rebellion with reference to slaves, so long and so far as not yet repealed, modified, or held void by Congress or by decision of the Supreme Court, and that I will, in like manner, abide by and faithfully support all proclamations of the President made during the existing rebellion having reference to slaves, so long and so far as not modified or declared void by decision of the Supreme Court; so help me God.
>
> Sworn and subscribed to before, _____, this _____ day of _____, 186_.

At the same time, General Grant also ordered that captured Confederate deserters be disarmed, fed, and given passes, passage on military railroads or steamers, and rations to carry them home. Southern deserters could be hired and were exempt from military service.[8]

Most of the men from Company A didn't join Wright and the others. Eight of them were later exchanged, and one was paroled, in addition to those who died. The decision to switch sides was not an easy one, or one made lightly. Even those who were reluctant or against the war considered those who switched sides to be dishonorable deserters, a legacy that followed them home and lasted in some cases for many generations.

Tar Heels had been hesitant to join the war, and many of the firebrands in power had been disinclined to place the state's natives in high-ranking generalships because of questions of loyalty to the cause. Confederates had plenty of reasons for switching sides. Some were genuinely pro-Union, others were psychologically or physically unable to handle prison life, some simply were willing to do whatever it took to survive, and others planned to escape or desert their new postings. Wright and his newly galvanized troopers were mustered into the First Regiment, Company F, of the United States Volunteer Infantry for a three-year enlistment. Boon and Braswell were assigned to Company C of the same regiment, and Matthews to Company D. Officers from New England drilled them until one proudly stated they had become a "first class body of soldiers."[9]

The regiment's first assignment was in Norfolk, Virginia, in April 1864. In late July Wright and the others were sent on a raid into Elizabeth City, North Carolina, just 119 miles east of Nashville. The effects and damage were ineffective, and Union leadership, perhaps aside from moral reasons, had second thoughts about keeping galvanized troops in the South. Men would be unlikely to want to fight their neighbors, or damage the world they'd eventually return to; desertion numbers would also certainly rise as units stayed in familiar territory. This was not to mention the danger to any rebel who might be captured—they would be considered deserters and traitors and, depending on the captors, could face severe punishment or execution. "It is not right," Grant said, "to expose them where, to be taken prisoners, they must surely suffer as deserters."[10]

Wright and Company F worked brief stints on provost duty (military police) in Norfolk and Portsmouth, Virginia.

The First Regiment boarded a steamer for New York City on August 15, as Grant decided to send the troops out west to maintain the Indian frontier. From there they boarded trains to Chicago, the last jumping-off point. On arrival two companies were sent to St. Louis, and the other four, including Wright's Company F, were dispatched to Camp Reno, Milwaukee. (Note: Some sources refer to this as Fort Reno, but there was another camp by that name near Washington DC. At other times, Camp Reno was known as Camp Holton and Camp Sigel.)

Wright could have surely served out the war in relative safety, paid, well fed, and well supplied. But as much as he was a reluctant Confederate, he had no interest in killing Indians or fellow Southerners. Instead he drew his pay on August 31 and made plans to walk out of camp. He wasn't alone in his plans. Leonard Coltraine, formerly of the Sixth North Carolina, and Cyrus Nance of the Twenty-Second North Carolina, both from Randolph County; William Hurst from Georgia; and Jacob Fisher, a former Bohemian immigrant from the First Virginia Cavalry, plotted along with him. Wright and the other men didn't waste much time in seizing their opportunity. Despite being hundreds of miles from home, and the South, and the war, they deserted on September 14. Wright carried with him his very accurate Enfield 1853 .577 caliber rifle and "equipments complete," a knapsack, a haversack, a canteen, a "pair" of scales, a bugle, insignia (an I and an F), and knapsack straps, valued at $28.02, according to the federal quartermaster.[11]

Suddenly Wright found himself in the odd situation of being wanted by two armies on charges of desertion and theft. Justice could be meted out upon capture by any unit of either army, home guards, or bounty hunters. The stakes were high; back home in North Carolina, in early 1864, some former Confederates who had joined the Union Army were captured by men under the command of Gen. George Pickett, who had been sent to the New Bern area after his disaster at Gettysburg. Some of the prisoners were released, but a big show was made when twenty-two of them were hanged near Kinston, which nearly escalated into a tit for tat with rightfully enraged Union commanders. Many considered this a war crime.

At this point Wright's whereabouts were unknown for several weeks. He kept no diaries or journals. There is no documentation to support it, but most likely he hid during the day and moved at night to avoid search parties, partisans, and everyday citizens who might report or take shots at him. His path perhaps would have been due south through Illinois and southern Indiana to reach more friendly surroundings in Kentucky. At that point he could have moved with Rangers or other irregulars across the state to Tennessee and then back into Virginia. He no doubt slept in the woods and barns, scavenged, and probably got handouts from sympathizers. He looked over his shoulder constantly. Again, his survival instinct would have carried him through unfamiliar terrain, often hostile, where anything from a misunderstanding with a farmer to an encounter with an aggressive Home Guard unit, or even crossing paths with regulars from either side could have easily ended with him on the wrong end of a rope hanging from a tree. Once in the South, he likely acquired passes to move safely through lines to return to his unit. There is the possibility that he went north into Canada, connected with rebel agents, and took a blockade runner into Wilmington, but this path seems highly unlikely at that stage of the war, given the effectiveness of the federal blockade. There were cases of escaped Confederates doing this, but neither the time frame nor other factors support this for Wright. Regardless, he was a long way from escaping the war, and farther still from home.

The Forty-Seventh Continues On

In November Lincoln visited Gettysburg and gave his address. In February Pickett, who had been sent to the New Bern/Kinston area, tried and failed to wrest New Bern from Union hands. In March Grant took over command of the Union forces and ended the prisoner exchange system, cutting off the cycle of Southern reinforcements.

After Bristoe Station, General Kirkland was back in command of the Forty-Seventh, along with Colonel Faribault. It was a quiet but tough winter at Orange Court House in Virginia. Ruffin Batchelor transferred out of the Forty-Seventh and into the Thirtieth North Carolina, which had plenty of Batchelor cousins among its ranks. In May the regiment was involved in several skirmishes before being assimilated into Gen. John R. Cooke's brigade in the Wilderness in Virginia, near where Stonewall Jackson had been mortally wounded. Gen. James Longstreet was supposed to relieve them but didn't show up, and there was disorganization within the ranks, which resulted in heavy losses of killed and wounded.

May 10, at the Battle of Wait's Shop, the regiment lost twenty more men before seeing just minor action on May 12 at Spotsylvania Court House; however, for the next fifteen days, they were constantly under fire.

On June 1, at the Battle of Bethesda Church, the Forty-Seventh held its ground behind breastworks, allowing the enemy to get within fifty yards before opening fire. The ensuing firefight was a rout, and Captain Thorp and the men of Company A, employed as sharpshooters, harassed the retreating Union men for two miles. From there the main body of men was sent to Cold Harbor in June, where General Kirkland was wounded, and Gen. William MacRae took over. Again the Forty-Seventh took heavy casualties of both killed and wounded, including Lt. George W. Westray. By nightfall the men found themselves surrounded by the enemy, but they managed to sneak away under cover of the dark.

From there the men marched. First they went to Gaines Mill, then crossed the Chickahominy River, and in mid-June crossed the James River and the Appomattox River. They were the extreme right of Lee's army and traveled thirty-five miles to Hatcher's Run, where Grant had broken Lee's lines. In the middle of the month Ruffin's new unit, the Thirtieth, engaged in the Battle of Snicker's Gap (also known as the Battle of Cool Spring) in Clarke County, Virginia. Although he was wounded five times, Ruffin managed to carry on eastward with his regiment.

In July the Forty-Seventh recrossed the Appomattox and then went on to Petersburg. The Battle of the Crater took place on July 30. Each engagement saw the numbers of the Forty-Seventh continue to drop. At the Battle of Reams Station on August 25, the men never fired; instead they overran the Union troops, taking flags, cannon, and 2,100 prisoners in close fighting. Losses in Company A were particularly bad.

On September 30 Heth attacked near Pegram House, and about a month later the Forty-Seventh took heavy losses again, this time at Burgess Mill. Numbers and morale were dropping precipitously as winter set in.

Wright Rejoins His Unit

By the winter 1864, it had become apparent the war was spiraling to an end. Atlanta had been burned, and Sherman was on the move, headed toward North Carolina. The only hope for the South at the end of the year was to continue long enough to force a war-weary North to seek favorable terms. The slaves in the South had been freed, all ports were blockaded, food and supplies were short, and inflation was devastating the civilian population.

For the average farmer there was little logic in rejoining the side for which defeat seemed eminent. Surely the thought to take a right turn and head back to Nash County must have crossed Wright's mind constantly as he neared the Southland. What stopped him? The evidence shows that he was an independent, stubborn man. Clearly he fit in with most of his fellow citizens and had little to gain by returning to arms. I suppose in the end that Wright was thinking less about the fight left in the war than what type of fight might be left after the war. He had marched off to war as an honorable man in his community, and now he was half a continent away wearing blue. That had been necessary to survive. However, should he manage to return home, those he would deal with when it came time to sell crops, seek help, or get his children in school might not hold the same view. Wright must have considered these things as he hid during the day and moved at night. It is unclear how long Wright and his fellow deserters stayed together, but it is likely they split up relatively soon for two reasons: it would have been harder to keep a low profile as a group, and Wright was the only one to return to his unit. He managed to walk all the way to Petersburg, Virginia, twenty-three miles south of Richmond. He joined his old unit in the trenches on or around October 31.[12]

The lingering question is, of course, why Wright headed right back into battle instead of turning south and back to White Oak and his farm and family. The desertion rate was rising in the Confederate ranks, and letters of despair from wives and families made it worse. Was he concerned about desertion penalties? The Home Guard? Fallout from neighbors after the war? Surely as a Union infantryman he would have known the direction of the war, and that the total collapse and defeat of the South was at hand. Perhaps he calculated in his mind that his odds of marching out the final days of the war were better than continuing to dodge pickets. Maybe he had joined up with another troop and there wasn't opportunity to exit. Wright did not pass the story on. A year after Bristoe Station, he found himself a private in the Confederate Army once again, peering out of the trenches of Petersburg at the Union guns sieging the city.

The winter of 1864 and early 1865 offered "some degree of comfort," Thorp recorded, as the men took solace in religious meetings, and those with money managed to attend the theater on occasion. Camp life was hard and sad, and with few left in Company A or the Forty-Seventh, many Confederates saw the end and deserted, some joining the Union Army as Wright had. Bone wrote in his memoir that as the war went into its later stages, chapel services became popular as "men were beginning to see the evils of war and were open to preaching. It seemed that it was often the case that the men who claimed a hope would be killed and sinner spared longer to have another opportunity for repentance."[13]

The end of the war was in sight for many, and Lincoln stepped up efforts to bring an end without further bloodshed. He presented a plan to pay $400 million to the slave states if they would quit the war by April 1. His cabinet rejected the plan outright, and while the price tag was enormous for the time, it no doubt would have drawn serious interest from states such as North Carolina.

In February the Union moved to try to sever communications and cut supply lines between rebel armies at Petersburg. There were nine wagon roads and five railroad connections in Petersburg, the second largest city in Virginia.[14] The lines of earthworks and trenches around Petersburg had started in 1862. Soldiers on both sides had been firing from opposing trenches that were fortified with sharpened stakes and included little built-in caves or "bomb-proofs" that offered cover from artillery. In July 1864 the Battle of the Crater took place when Union troops under Lt. Col. Henry Pleasants filled a mineshaft under the Confederate lines with explosives and detonated it. Casualties were horrific, and when it was all done, a months-long siege and standoff was in place.

The Forty-Seventh was part of the action that stopped Union troops, again taking casualties. In March 1865 the lines broke. Company A was moved to the rear and spent most of its time holding off skirmishers. Captain Thorp was named as the replacement to command the sharpshooters in the Forty-Seventh and received high praise from General McRae, who said of Thorp, "he will do as much fighting and talk as little of it as any officer in our army."[15] In April they came to the rescue of a Florida regiment that had been overrun by Union cavalry, and things got worse from there. Thirty men of the Forty-Seventh held off an estimated one hundred skirmishers near Southerland Station, turning back two charges before being nearly annihilated in the third. Thorp noted that "only a few came out," and the men had no way to cross the river.[16] Gen. A. P. Hill was killed at the third Battle of Petersburg. The desertion of Confederates over to Union lines was high, and many of the men in the ranks felt that the surrender of the Army of Northern Virginia should have taken place at Petersburg.

Lee had to abandon Petersburg, even though it meant Richmond would fall. He sent word to President Davis, who got the message in church that he needed to flee the city—other parishioners realized what was going on, and a mob of people began a mass exodus.[17] Richmond surrendered. The Confederate Army and the war in general simply became a survival game, a prolonging of the inevitable. It was clear negotiations for a settled peace or any option other than a return to the Union was impossible. For most of North Carolina and its people, they had never been in favor of the war to begin with, and they wanted to get home and rebuild their lives. It was a long slog of despair from Petersburg to Appomattox, and in the skirmishes along the way; no doubt the men prayed they would not be among the last men killed for a Lost Cause.

Wright's reunion with his brother in the trenches at Petersburg was cut short when Ruffin was captured on April 3 after fierce fighting on April 2, which resulted in the Forty-Seventh being "defeated, slain, wounded, captured, or scattered."[18] Ruffin may have been swept up in the enormous numbers of rebels who simply collapsed by the roadside and waited to be captured by the pressing Union cavalry, as he was surely still suffering from the wounds at Snickers Gap. He was sent to the prison camp at Hart's Island, New York, on April 17 and wasn't released until two months after Lee surrendered and he finally took the Oath of Allegiance. Wright reeled back with what little remained of his unit.

Morale had bottomed out in the Confederate Army long before. Sam Watkins, author of the well-written and authentic chronicle of the common soldier's plight *Company Aytch*, said this of the attitude: "We cursed the war, we cursed [Gen. Braxton] Bragg, we cursed the Southern Confederacy. All our pride and valor had gone, and we were sick of war and the Southern Confederacy."[19]

In early April they passed through Amelia Court House and then Farmville. They got rations from the government store, which was running so short that on one distribution, the men got only two ears of corn each. They had hoped to find more rations but instead found ammunition, a bitter irony. Lee had hoped to take the railroad to Danville, but Gen. Phil Sheridan cut them off, so they changed direction and headed toward Lynchburg on April 5.[20] On the evening of April 7 they rushed to the battlefield where Gen. Fitzhugh Lee's cavalry was engaged with Gen. David Gregg's cavalry. Gregg was captured, and the attack stopped. That same day Grant contacted Lee and on April 8 offered a "restoration of peace."[21]

On Palm Sunday, April 9, the Forty-Seventh finally arrived at Appomattox, expecting a fight. They were put into the line, but General McRae called a halt, dismounted, and lay down, as did the men. Some of Lee's advisers suggested the men take to the countryside and continue to fight as guerillas. At that point the Forty-Seventh had no field officer and only two captains: Faucette of Company K and Thorp of Company A. All that remained of Company A were five sergeants, Wright, Thorp, and eleven other men. Company D had only three men.

Finally, when Grant and Lee met in the parlor of Wilmer McLean's farmhouse, the war ended for the men of the Forty-Seventh. There weren't many of them left, just seventy-seven. Company A consisted of eleven privates and two sergeants besides Sgt. Maj. P. A. Page, 2nd Sgt. W. E. Stott, and 3rd Sgt. W. M. Warren, along with Cpl. W. H. Perry. There were 2,400 cavalry in Lee's army who refused to surrender and rode off. Thorp was poignant and eloquent in his description of how he and his colleagues were treated: "Highest respect shown by U.S. Soldiers . . . they showed marked consideration for our feelings. If the whole country could have witnessed this sympathetic scene between the Old Greys and the Old Blues, seas of bitter tears and mountains of hate would have been spared."[22]

Grant's terms were generous: the officers and men were allowed to go home "not to be disturbed by U.S. authority so long as they observe their paroles and the laws in force where they may reside," and the men were even allowed to keep their horses. This set the precedent that the rebels were not be charged with treason.[23]

The Confederates were given a herd of fat young steers and had the most food they had seen in some time. On Monday and Tuesday they received company, and on Wednesday they were paroled. They formed organization for the last time and marched between open ranks of the Union Army. There were 28,231 men paroled, including Wright, who stacked arms, including his newly acquired Enfield. There was no federal officer in sight, and no music. The men broke ranks to go their separate ways. Wright was mustered out of the Confederate Army on April 9, 1865.

"Boys, I have done the best I could for you. Go home now. And if you make as good citizens as you have soldiers, you will do well, and I shall be most proud of you. Goodbye, and God bless you all," General Lee told the men.[24]

Grant perhaps gave a more blunt and accurate assessment. "I felt . . . sad and depressed at the downfall of a foe who had fought so long and valiantly, and had suffered so much for a cause, though the cause was, I believe, one of the worst for which a people ever fought."[25] Clearly, he was referring to slavery.

In other units, and states, many wanted to continue to fight as guerrillas or go to Mexico. The Forty-Seventh was done. The brigade was 83 percent farmers, and their thoughts had long turned to getting home, reuniting with wives and children, and trying to get a crop in the ground. Most of them were poor, and the Forty-Seventh had 111 men who served as substitutes. Of the 1,589 who had entered the war, 977 had become casualties, and 20 had been either temporarily or permanently galvanized. North Carolina had 31,954 men killed, including 343 from Nash, 423 from Edgecombe, 368 from Franklin, and 355 from Wilson. Five Nash County men serving in the U.S. Colored Troops died.

Wright wanted to see his wife and children and get back to his farm, get back to his life. He had survived against tremendous odds, not just bullets and bayonets but overwhelming disease and sickness. He was tough, prematurely aged, and battered, but first and foremost, he was a survivor. The Nash County man turned south for another long walk, but this time he was headed home to a people and place he'd spent more than three years trying to defend, his cause mixed with others, all of them lost.

10

Return and Reconstruction

Nations, like individuals, are punished for their transgressions.

—Gen. ULYSSES S. GRANT

I am not ashamed of having fought on the side of slavery—a
soldier fights for his country—right or wrong—he is not
responsible for the political merits of the course he fits in.

—Col. JOHN S. MOSBY

Most of the men in the Army of Northern Virginia had not been
paid in more than twelve months, but with high inflation and virtually worthless Confederate scrip, it mattered little. Many of the
North Carolinians, including the Nash County men across various
regiments, decided to walk home in groups. Based on the time line,
geography, relationships, and practicality, it's likely Wright walked
home in a group of men that included John Wesley Bone, although
Bone recorded no names of his fellow travelers in his memoir.
They were in different companies, but Wright and Bone were both
from Nashville. The officers instructed the veterans to ask people
of means for something to eat on their journey home, but if they
were refused, to take what they needed and try to treat the provid-
ers with respect.[1] No rank or command was assumed among the
men; the ragtag remnants of the army were once again neighbors
and farmers and laborers, men anxious to get home to wives and
children and what they hoped would be homes still standing. Some

had nothing to return to; many of those at home had no idea when their loved ones would return, if ever.

They departed Virginia on the Tuesday after Lee surrendered. On the first night the group of about eighteen to twenty men stopped at the home of a Baptist preacher who shared his food but told the men that the Yankees had taken most of what he had.

The next day, Wednesday, the men got milk and bread at the home of a widow whose son had just returned home. She told the group that she was thankful that her boy survived and would provide for them as she hoped someone else would have provided for her child. The group crossed the Richmond and Danville Railroad line around dark and ironically managed to get supper and a room at the local poor house/county home.

Two days later, on Friday, the men got an early start, and the group started to scatter, as some headed due south, while others turned east. They passed through Marysville and on Saturday reached Taylor's Ferry on the Roanoke River, which is about four miles north of the North Carolina line in Mecklenburg County, Virginia. Bone said that the group crossed "on a ferry run by two Negroes" who charged a dollar a head, which must have made for an uncomfortable exchange—recently freed slaves encountering what had to appear as a roving band of rebel soldiers, only days removed from the battlefield. There are many accounts of discharged Confederates turning into gangs or bands of thieves, robbing and resorting to violence in the chaotic weeks and months after the war wound down. Plus the war was technically not yet over, despite Lee's surrender. After crossing, rain set in, and the ex-Confederates sought shelter in an abandoned house.

On Sunday the men passed through Warrenton, North Carolina, and stopped at the farm of former quartermaster Maj. Buck Williams and were given supper and a room by the foreman. Close to home, they set out early and were given breakfast by a farmer and his wife, the parents of a surgeon from the Twenty-Second North Carolina, who had just gotten home the night before. By late evening the men arrived in Nash County, near Portis (Bone refers to it as Porter's) Gold Mine close to Hilliardston. The group split here again, and Bone noted that some came to realize they "had nowhere to go." Those who were left stayed with former county sheriff Thomas Cooper.[2] The next day they passed through Nashville, and by early afternoon Wright was making his way down the road, and back to his family and home and comforts he'd not seen in years. The only certainty ahead was a host of questions and unknowns.

The End of the War

When Sherman entered North Carolina, he ordered restraint from the men, unlike the devastation that had been wreaked on the rest of the South. Fayetteville, home of the arsenal that was seized at the beginning of hostilities, was burned, but things were different.

"Our men seemed to understand that they were entering a state which has suffered for its Union sentiment, and whose inhabitants would greatly embrace the old flag again if they can have the opportunity," wrote one of Sherman's staff officers.[3]

After General Sherman and General Johnston clashed in a bloody meeting at Bentonville in Johnston County, about fifty miles south of Raleigh on April 11, Johnston retreated north, passing through Raleigh and Durham's Station (at the time, just a rail stop between Raleigh and Greensboro; later it became Durham, one of the state's largest cities) as he headed to Greensboro. Governor Zebulon Vance hadn't committed to a surrender but sent a flag of truce to Sherman to try and save Raleigh. Many historians believe that North Carolina's "disloyal reputation" saved the capital and the state from the mass destruction wrought by Sherman on his campaign. Former governor, U.S. senator, U.S. vice presidential candidate, U.S. secretary of the navy, and then Confederate senator William A. Graham urged Vance to try to negotiate a separate peace with Sherman and leave the CSA out of the equation. Vance agreed and sent Graham and former governor and UNC president David Swain to meet with Sherman, but before they could talk, the mayor of Raleigh surrendered the city.[4] Johnston stopped at Durham's Station and sent a messenger to Sherman to discuss terms and put "a stop to the needless sacrifice of life." Lincoln was assassinated two days later.

Davis wanted to continue to conscript soldiers and keep fighting, while the general called the idea "inexpressibly wild" that anyone who carried hope that the Confederacy could still win and stated that "it would be of the greatest of human crimes to continue the war." Gen. P. G. T. Beauregard agreed, realizing that Davis sought negotiations, not surrender.[5]

Sherman was met at the train station in Raleigh by Union troops who urged him not to accept Johnston's surrender. A few thousand marched to the city and had to be stopped by Gen. John A. Logan. They wanted to continue to punish the Confederates. When Sherman told Johnston about the assassination, Johnston went into a panic, fearing Sherman would blame the Confederate government, and Johnston called Booth's act "a disgrace to the age." Johnston wanted to surrender his army and all the rest of the troops in the CSA. He summoned former U.S. vice president and current CSA secretary of war John C. Breckinridge, who wanted amnesty for Davis and the rest of the cabinet. Sherman advised Breckinridge that the lot of them should flee the country.[6]

On April 17 they sat down at the 350-acre farm of James Bennett in Durham to discuss terms of surrender that would end the war. Johnston got word of Lee's surrender but withheld the information from his men while he sought good terms. Sherman was generous, and although he'd told his superiors he would offer the same terms Grant gave Lee at Appomattox, he attempted to end the war on conciliatory terms. This is the agreement they signed on April 18:

> Memorandum or basis of agreement made this 18th day of April, A.D. 1865, near Durham's Station, in the state of North Carolina, by and between General Joseph E. Johnston . . . and Maj. Gen. William T. Sherman. . . .
>
> First. The Contending armies now in the field to maintain the status quo until notice is given by the commanding general of any one to its opponent. . . .
>
> Second. The Confederate armies now in existence to be disbanded and conducted to their several State capitals, there to deposit

their arms and public property in the State Arsenal, and each officer and man to execute and file an agreement to cease from acts of war and to abide by the action of both State and Federal authority. . . .

Third. The recognition by the Executive of the United States, of the several State governments, of their officers and legislatures taking the oaths prescribed by the Constitution of the United States, and where conflicting state governments have resulted from the war the legitimacy of all shall be submitted to the [U.S.] Supreme Court.

Fourth. The re-establishment of all the Federal courts in the several States, with powers as defined by the Constitution and laws of Congress.

Fifth. The people and inhabitants of all the States to be guaranteed, so far as the Executive can, their political rights and franchises, as well as their rights of person and property, as defined by the [U.S.] Constitution and of the States respectively.

Sixth. The Executive authority of the Government of the United States not to disturb any of the people by reason of the late war so long as they live in peace and quiet, abstain from acts of armed hostility, and obey the laws . . . at the place of their residence.

Seven. In general terms, the war to cease, a general amnesty, so far as the Executive of the United States can command, on condition of the disbandment of the Confederate armies . . . and the resumption of peaceful pursuits by the officers and men hitherto composing said armies.[7]

President Andrew Johnson and the cabinet were furious and rejected the deal. Secretary of War Stanton sent Grant to Durham to refuse the surrender, relieve Sherman, and continue the fight if necessary. The memo they issued was sent to the papers, and Sherman was vilified across the North for being soft, some even offering the ridiculous sentiment that the man who set the South on fire and ended the war was a traitor. The cabinet feared the terms would restore "rebel authority" and allow them to re-establish slavery. The memo stated the agreement "formed no poises of a true and lasting peace, but relieved rebels from the pressure of our victories and left them in condition to overthrow the United States Government."[8]

Grant arrived on April 24 to deliver the news that embarrassed and angered Sherman. He was ordered to give Johnston forty-eight hours to accept the amended terms "instant, purely and simply," or hostilities would resume. Davis sent orders to Johnston to disband the army and send them to the mountains, and to dispatch a cavalry escort for Davis to use to escape. Johnston refused the orders.

Both Sherman and Johnston were in difficult spots. Confederate morale was terrible, the troops were concerned about being POWs, and Johnston and his generals feared a complete breakdown. Between April 19 and April 24, thousands of men deserted, some leaving with the army's mules and horses. It's been written often that the discontent of the rebel soldiers played as large a role as Sherman's army in forcing the surrender. Johnston considered disbanding the army on the spot to prevent Union troops from devastating the countryside in pursuit. In making his case to Secretary of War John Breckinridge, he wrote, "We have to save the people, spare the blood of the army and save the high civil functionaries." He remarked later, "Commanders believe the troops will not fight again." Sherman was worried that if the army disbanded they could form into bands of guerrillas, and there would be anarchy. He wrote as much in a letter to his wife Ellen: "That is what I most fear. Such men as Wade Hampton, [Nathan B.] Forrest, Wirt Adams, etc., never will work and nothing is left for them but death or highway robbery."[9]

This time it was Johnston who rejected the terms of surrender, because it provided for no food, shelter, or money for his bedraggled troops. As the two generals struggled, Union general John Schofield suggested they draft and sign two agreements. One, with the Appomattox terms and additional amendments to satisfy Johnston, and another with simply the Appomattox terms—one way or another, both Sherman and Johnston were determined to end the war. Schofield's amendments allowed for the Confederates to keep their transportation, and for each brigade to retain weapons equal to about one-seventh of the total number of men, which would be surrendered to local authorities when the men returned home. There was a realistic fear that men returning home would be subject to lawlessness and roving bands of rebels who had deserted or refused to surrender. The troops from Arkansas and Texas would get water transportation to Mobile or New Orleans. Schofield also arranged for 250,000 rations to be issued to Johnston's troops, in part to keep the defeated Confederates from stealing from their own people. The terms were signed on April 26.

While the Confederate Cabinet approved the terms, they did not authorize Johnston to surrender the entirety of the rebel forces, mostly because they wanted time to flee the country. Sherman had also been told that he could only end the campaign as it related to Johnston's force. Johnston surrendered ninety thousand troops in North Carolina, South Carolina, Georgia, and Florida. John Mosby had disbanded his Rangers in Virginia a few days earlier, and in early May Gen. Richard Taylor and Gen. Nathan B. Forrest surrendered, and William Quantrill was killed. The last battle of the war was fought on May 13 at Palmetto Ranch, Texas, and Gen. Kirby Smith was the last to surrender on May 26.

Union soldiers picked the Bennett homestead clean, essentially looting and claiming souvenirs and spoils from the farm owners. Even though they were given receipts for some items taken, the Bennetts were never reimbursed by the government despite numerous appeals.

Chaos ensued as Jefferson Davis tried to talk several leaders into moving the Confederacy farther south or to Mexico, and some considered continuing a guerrilla war, but calmer heads prevailed. Davis met with the Confederate cabinet for the last time on May 5, where they disbanded the government. Davis and his wife Varina fled south but were captured on May 10 in Irwin County, Georgia. Davis was sent to prison and charged with treason; he was released after two years and pardoned by President Johnson on Christmas Day, 1868. In the end, no treason trials were held, although Davis wanted one so he could prove that secession was permissible under the Constitution. Johnson and the federal government wanted to avoid this and thought releasing Davis instead of prosecution and possible execution would aid reconciliation. While many decried the lack of justice, it was a wise solution, and the Supreme Court resolved the issue of the legality of secession in 1869, when it decided that states could not secede from the Union.

Governor Vance headed west to avoid federal authorities, but he was tracked down in Statesville and arrested in May on his thirty-first birthday. He was sent to Old Capitol Prison in Washington. He applied for a pardon in June and was released in July. He got an official pardon later in 1867, although he was never actually charged with a crime.

Putting the Union Back Together

President Johnson appointed William Woods Holden as provisional governor of North Carolina on May 29, 1865. Holden had made a bid for the office in 1864 against his former friend and ally Vance and had been rolled over 58,046–14,490, so his support from the populace was weak but perhaps better than appointees in some less internally conflicted states.[10] A week earlier Johnson issued a proclamation that granted amnesty to all Southerners who took an Oath of Allegiance to the U.S. Constitution. Holden immediately called for a convention to nullify the ordinance of secession, abolish slavery, restore the state to the Union, and repudiate the state's wartime debt. A convention drew up a document whereby slavery was abolished and the ordinance of secession was repealed, and it passed the 13th Amendment. However, voters ended up rejecting the new state constitution in 1866 and didn't approve one until 1868 when North Carolina rejoined the Union—the state was unable to receive federal funds until it was back in the Union, further compounding the hardships on common North Carolinians, and further evidencing the stubbornness of the people in power.

Holden lost to a former state senator and Vance's state treasurer, Jonathan Worth, in a special election later in 1865. Worth had sided with Holden in opposing the war during the secession talk all the way through to its conclusion and was a major supporter of the push for peace in 1864. However, many in the North viewed Holden's loss as a sign of disloyalty to the Union, and in December 1865 Congress refused to seat any Southerners.

In 1866 North Carolina passed "Black Codes" that prevented blacks from voting and from having equal legal rights, and along with other Southern states it rejected the 14th Amendment. The Black Codes were aimed at retaining as many of the terms of slavery as possible, such as denying blacks the right to vote, serve on juries, or testify against whites. The codes allowed young blacks to be apprenticed to their former owners, established the death penalty for black men who raped white women, restricted the movement of blacks in and out of state, prohibited them from owning firearms without obtaining a permit one year in advance, and prohibited interracial marriages. Even at that level, North Carolina's Black Codes were considered mild compared to most other Southern states.

In June 1866, in Pulaski, Tennessee, a group of men met in the law office of Thomas M. Jones, a Person County, North Carolina, native, and formed a new fraternal-like organization. They borrowed their name from the Greek word *kuklos*, which means circle or band, and formed the Ku Klux Klan. They were in North Carolina by 1867. What started as pranks and parades escalated quickly into a vicious campaign of terror when politicians and vigilantes joined and set "new goals." The group offered a violent, intimidating, and criminal response to the duly elected blacks and Republicans in the legislature, and local groups of the KKK spread quickly. It was a secret group that terrorized blacks as well as whites who helped blacks. They committed heinous murders by shooting, hanging, or drowning their victims. The groups operated by using men from a nearby area to commit the acts, for which the favor was then returned. They did not operate in largely black populated areas, as they were also cowards.[11]

The Reconstruction Act of 1867 issued by Congress ended the president's plan and broke the South into military districts. North Carolina was placed into District 2 with South Carolina. Black Codes were thrown off the books.

Gen. Dan Sickles was placed in charge of the district. Sickles had been a rising political star until he shot and killed his wife's lover, the son of Francis Scott Key. Sickles quickly overreached his military authority and issued a series of General Orders to extend his power. They included subordinating state law to military law, including making military courts superior to civil and federal courts, and giving himself authority over local elections. He declared some elections invalid, quarantined ports, and ordered that no grain could be distilled to produce alcohol, that no mortgages could be foreclosed, and that no private debts that had accumulated from the time of South Carolina's secession through May 15, 1865, could be collected. North Carolina officials were particularly outraged about the latter as the state had remained in the Union an additional five months after the Fort Sumter attack.[12] Reconstruction would be far worse than anything Lincoln or Johnson had in mind.

The Republican Party in North Carolina was one of the two largest in the South, in both numbers and proportion of whites. The party consisted of native whites, who some locals referred to as "scalawags," as well as Unionists, small farmers, old Whigs, Holden fans, and people who wanted to appease the North. Blacks and carpetbaggers (those from the North who went to the South after the war to gain money or fame) made up the rest of the party.

Former governor Holden broke with Johnson in 1867 and became a Radical Republican. He ran against Thomas Samuel Ashe in 1868 and won. The state constitution was passed that year and abolished slavery, allowed for universal suffrage (for men), eliminated all property requirements for office (but did not allow atheists to be candidates), allowed for the popular election of state and county officials, abolished the county court system, required public schools to be open at least four months per year, and created the new offices of lieutenant governor, superintendent of public works, and superintendent of public instruction. Ulysses S. Grant carried the vote for president in 1868, by a 96,000–84,000 vote count.

Holden took on the Ku Klux Klan full force, hiring detectives to track down members and calling out the militia in 1870. Klan members were arrested, and habeas corpus was suspended with the Shoffner Act. This was known as the Kirk-Holden War, after George Washington Kirk, who was hired to handle the matter. Martial law was declared in Caswell and Alamance Counties after Wyatt Outlaw, a black town official and constable, was lynched in Graham, an Alamance County town located between Raleigh and Greensboro. A man who claimed to know the identities of the murderers was found dead shortly afterward. John W. Stephens, a white Republican popular with blacks in Caswell County, was killed by the KKK in the courthouse. Authorities indicted 1,400 men during the campaign, but Holden's administration was doomed. The Democratic Party regained control of the House that year and impeached, convicted, and removed Holden from office, the first time that had happened in U.S. history. The Shoffner Act was repealed, and secret political and military societies were outlawed. The Klan virtually disappeared in North Carolina for half a century, other than some sporadic activity in Cleveland and Rutherford Counties.

Many North Carolinians lost their land or had to sell at a reduced price after the war when the economy collapsed. There were 331,000 recently freed slaves and previously freed blacks in North Carolina after the war. Many slaves who didn't commandeer plantations were left homeless or forced into manual labor and sharecropping.

Wright Batchelor returned to his previous position as superintendent of the Nash County Poor House in 1866, and instead of taking cash, he took his salary in half the crop grown by the residents. Jordan Vester was appointed overseer in 1867 with a salary of $325, two and a half barrels of corn, and 250 pounds of pork. Wright's old commanding officer, Capt. John Thorp, was one of the wardens in 1867, and Wright went on to serve on and off for years before essentially taking the job somewhat permanently for the rest of his life.

North Carolina saw the benefits almost immediately after rejoining the Union. The 1868 constitution was quickly ratified after a January to March convention, and in July the 14th Amendment was passed. The new constitution created the county commissioner system that is still in place and broke up the "courthouse rings" of justice of the peace elections by the state legislature, which essentially allowed those in Raleigh to appoint buddies and political cronies to offices that allowed them to control the entire state through

local bodies. The document also eliminated high property qualifica-
tions to hold office. For the first time blacks were eligible for public education in "separate but equal" facilities. There is no record
of a public school after the war in Nash County until 1872, when
138 white students and 84 black students attended class.

One of Wright's old lieutenants from the Forty-Seventh North
Carolina came home to serve as Rocky Mount's first mayor after it
was incorporated in April 1867 with three hundred residents. Benjamin H. Bunn joined the Confederate Army at age seventeen and
eventually made it to captain in the Forty-Seventh. Bunn studied
at local schools, where one of his teachers was future fellow officer John H. Thorp. Bunn's brother William was killed at the Battle
of Burgess Mill in October 1864, and another brother, Elias, died
from his wounds at Hanover Courthouse. Bunn was with the Forty-
Seventh at Gettysburg, the Wilderness, Spotsylvania, Gaines Mill,
Reams Station, Burgess Mill, and Petersburg, so much of his time
in the unit was while Wright was a POW or in the Union Army, but
they knew each other. Bunn was wounded at Gettysburg and again
at Petersburg and was evacuated to Richmond. When Petersburg
fell, he got out of bed and walked to Danville.[13] He was put on a
train and sent back to Rocky Mount, where he arrived the day of
the unit's surrender at Appomattox.[14] He got his law license in 1866
and began a successful career as a noted speaker and powerful man
to have on one's side in a court proceeding. An area in present-day
Rocky Mount is named after his home, Benvenue.

Rocky Mount elected a Radical Republican mayor in 1878, Spen-
cer Fountain. He was a supporter of Holden's but had been in favor
of North Carolina leaving the Confederacy. In 1867 whites made up
30 percent of the Republican Party in North Carolina. They hoped
that biracial politics would allay racial fears about the black population in politics. Holden and other white Republicans, while tremendously progressive for the time period on race relations, were
only willing to go so far. They denied that political and social equal-
ity with blacks was the same thing. Freedmen were one thing, but
political power was another entirely. Very few North Carolinians
claimed to be Radicals, but Wright became a Republican and a Rad-

ical. People like him were racially moderate and saw themselves as stewards for prosperity, social stability, and the rule of the law, but they did not want to be perceived as upending racial hierarchy or the political and economic system. Many common and poor whites were disillusioned by the Democratic Party that had led them into war, and they viewed the party as beholden to railroad, banking, and industrial interests. While many former Confederate officers became politicians, the enlisted men returned to their former positions as poor farmers or laborers. This resentment helped fuel the Radical Republican/Fusionist movement.[15]

By 1870 all the rebellious states had returned to the Union. That year's census listed Wright as a farmer and as literate, a valuable skill he picked up during the war. It's likely that Thorp, the school-teacher, helped Wright and many like him. Sally Ann was listed as keeping house, the children and women as "at home," and the boys, including ten-year-old Bunnion, as farm laborers. Wright's mother-in-law, Lucy Ward, eighty, was living with the family, and a black farmhand, Frank Cooper, nineteen, was part of the household as well.

North Carolina was spared the worst infrastructure ravages of the war and within fifty years became the most industrialized state in the south. After 1870 tobacco, cotton, and corn took off as main crops, and by the 1880s many farmers were growing crops for market instead of for personal and family consumption. The prewar model of just laboring for survival was fading out.

As for Nash County, the population was right around 11,000 in 1870, after the natural drop following the war. Federal troops left the state in 1877. By 1880 that total had jumped to 17,731—a 60 percent growth spurt. Tobacco warehouses started becoming big in Goldsboro, Rocky Mount, Durham, Kinston, and Wilson.

Education was still sporadic as best, and most students who were enrolled were sent to private or tuition-charging schools (also called subscription schools). In 1869 Nash County there were schools in the townships of Union Hope, Battleboro, Nashville, Stanhope, and Hillardston. That number more than doubled by 1889. Literacy rates were abysmal but slowly improved. In 1871 the Southern Claims Commission was formed to investigate and reimburse Southern Unionists who had provided support and materiel during the war. The commission was quite busy in North Carolina, operating until 1880.

The 1880 census showed Wright as a farmer renting 200 acres, with ownership of 325 acres and property worth $7,000. Sally Ann was listed as owning 27 improved acres, 339 unimproved acres, and property with a cash value of $2,000. The couple owned $600 worth of livestock combined. The value of those assets would be over $200,000 today. Clearly the Batchelors were prospering. It also appears that a grandchild, Missouri Davis, seven, was living in the home. Ruffin was nearby with his own farm of 58 improved acres, 42 unimproved acres, and property of $800.

Wright was active in the community, and in 1881 he and Sally Ann and four other couples founded Elm Grove Baptist Church on the outskirts of Nashville. The group was granted "letters of dismission" from Pleasant Grove Baptist to plant the new church, which is still active today.[16]

Wright even decided to get into local politics as a scalawag. In August 1884 the *Goldsboro Messenger* reported on the county convention of the "Radicals of Nash" being held in Nashville. It was a lively crowd. "From clerk Morgan, we learn that the following were the nominations: For Coroner, Wright Batchelor; for Treasurer, Jas. Harper; for Register, J. J. Drake, when the time came to nominate a Sheriff, the convention broke up in a row." Wright lost that election by the close vote of 1,686–1,627. He never ran for office again.

II

Trouble about a "Yaller" Dog

Civil wars leave nothing but tombs.

—ALPHONSE DE LAMARTINE, French poet

By 1880 Reconstruction had ended, and things were looking up for the Batchelors. In addition to running his farm, Wright continued as superintendent of the county poor house. Eugenia, the oldest child, was twenty-seven and had given Wright and Sally Ann their first grandchild. Little Wright was six, and Little Sally Ann, born in 1866, was fourteen; Peter Ruffin, named after Wright's brother and best friend, came along the next fall in 1867. Nannie was born in 1870, and Jordan (my great-grandfather), born in 1872, was just two years older than Little Wright. The older children had already left home.

After dabbling in politics with his run for county coroner, Wright decided office holding was not for him. He stayed involved in the community and remained a Republican, and he was well respected. His job at the poor house gave him some notice as a community leader.

There were undoubtedly those in the community who did not appreciate the fact that Wright had donned Union blue, no matter how briefly or insincerely his service might have been, or the fact that he deserted. Most of his Nash County comrades in arms who had been captured chose to remain in prison rather than switch sides. And despite the fact that Wright had deserted the Union ranks and had returned to the front lines in Petersburg instead of going home, some wondered whether he was still "one of them." After all, he had joined the Radical Republicans, who supported rights for blacks and were ready to put the war and its horrific legacy behind them. Wright was, by definition, a "scalawag," a white Southerner who joined with Republicans. His thoughts on race would surely have been unpopular with many fellow citizens who now viewed freed slaves as competition in the labor and farm markets. While it is unlikely that any man in Nash County considered blacks and whites to be equal, Wright certainly would have been considered peculiar and would have faced some resentment from his peers. Even in a reluctant Confederate state, there were plenty of hardliners. Former slaves and even freedmen, as well as those who attempted to help them, were easy targets.

There was at least one family that apparently had some issues with Wright Batchelor, the Rackleys. Lemon "Big Lem" Rackley was a Confederate veteran who served in the Twelfth North Carolina regiment and was a successful planter with several hundred acres outside Nashville after the war. Big Lem was captured near Winchester, Virginia, sent to Point Lookout after Wright had departed as a Union private, and surely knew of his neighbor's exploits. Rackley declined the oath and stayed in the camp until exchanged in March 1865. There is no recorded evidence of a prior dispute, but the circumstances that unfolded in 1886 indicate there certainly had to be some kind of bad blood brewing below the surface between the Batchelors and the Rackleys.

Big Lem's son, twenty-two-year-old Lemon (sometimes listed as Lemuel) "Little Lem" Tolliver Rackley, worked on the family farm and owned a dog who often rambled the countryside, including the nearby poor house property. Theories both oral and written vary on what specifically heated up tensions, but certainly at the center was a "yaller" (yellow) dog.

At least one modern source (my longtime friend Terry) speculated that Rackley's dog "pissed on Wright's [or the Poor House's] tobacco crop," which had been cured and taken to Nashville to be sold. This would have rendered the crop unsalable and would have been a financial disaster. It is more likely, as relayed through passed down stories, that poultry was the problem. Wright noticed that chickens on the farm were disappearing on a regular basis. He decided one night that he would stand guard over the livestock and set an ambush for the culprit. As it turned out, the chicken thief was Rackley's "yaller" dog. Wright's skills with a rifle were as sharp as they had ever been, and in the form of country justice that still exists today in many rural areas, he dispatched the dog that night and ended the disruption in the poor house food supply.[1]

Little Lem was furious when he discovered the fate of his companion and was determined that he would confront Batchelor over the issue. His anger had not subsided days later, and he knew he could find Wright in Nashville, as the older man had regular business at the courthouse.

November 4, 1886, was an overcast day with the crispness of fall setting in. The crops were out of the fields, and people were preparing for winter. Wright's duties as poor house superintendent brought him to the county courthouse that afternoon, which was located on Main Street (now called Washington Street), about a block away from its current location. It was in the center of downtown and quite a busy place.

Having completed his necessary paperwork, Wright was perhaps headed to purchase a few supplies, or maybe settle some credit accounts for himself or the poor house. He was on his way down the steps when his neighbor, Little Lem, still aggrieved over the killing of his dog, stepped out from a nearby building, likely the Grand Jury Building next door. He confronted my great-great-granddaddy and started yelling. No one paid much attention until suddenly Rackley pulled out a "five shilling [dollar] pistol" from under his jacket, raised it with his right hand, and pointed it at Wright's head. Wright, most certainly armed himself, was perhaps shocked but could not imagine that the younger man intended to fire. He didn't make a move for his weapon.

Unsatisfied, or maybe angry at what the straightforward Wright said, Rackley continued to point the pistol, adjusted his aim from point blank range, and pulled the trigger. The cracking sound of the shot echoed off the old brick facade of the courthouse and down the street, and while the shouting had garnered the attention of a few, gunfire drew all eyes, and gasps and shouts followed. Wright crumpled to the ground, grasping at his throat, with a wound three inches wide and three inches deep in the left side of his neck. He was dead before he hit the steps. Rackley, perhaps shocked at his own lack of control and the heated escalation, looked around and took off running as bystanders now rushed futilely to aid Batchelor, and others chased after his assailant.

The court charges would later read that Rackley had "feloniously willfully and of his malice aforethought did shoot & discharge . . . the leaden bullet aforesaid out of the pistol."[2]

At just fifty-eight years old Wright Stephen Batchelor, who had survived Pickett's Charge, Bristoe Station, a federal prison camp, a brief Indian campaign, two armies, bounty hunters and home guards, the siege of Petersburg, and the walk home from Appomattox, was dead. There was chaos in the street as numerous locals witnessed the whole scene devolve in seconds.

Six of those witnesses would later testify to the grand jury: J. H. Collins, C. W. Ward, G. W. Strickland, Emerson Batchelor, May Batchelor, and Thomas Stallings. Within twenty-four hours Nash County Sheriff J. P. Arrington caught up with and took Rackley into custody without incident.

There are a couple of possibilities here, considering the steps young Rackley took in shooting down a man in the middle of the day at the busiest thoroughfare in town: there was more involved than a chicken-killing dog, or Rackley was a mentally unstable hothead.

A few days later Wright was laid to rest in Sally Ann's family cemetery. Instead of spending his last years farming and directing the poor house, marrying off children, and spinning tales for a large audience of grandchildren about how he'd dodged Yankee bullets for three years, his life had been cut short just a few miles from home. Sally Ann was heartbroken and devastated.

Local solicitor D. Worthington wasted no time in convening a grand jury for the case of *The State of North Carolina v. Lem Rackley Jr.* in what looked to be a clear, open-and-shut case of first-degree, premeditated murder. The suspect had planned the attack, hidden and waited for his victim, and shot him in broad daylight in front of countless witnesses. It was cold-blooded murder in a scene from the mythical Wild West.

A True Bill of Indictment was issued in Superior Court in Nash County in the November 1886 term, from the Grand Jury Foreman W. C. Taylor.

While court records and transcripts reveal very few details of trials in nineteenth-century Nash County cases, what was there was nothing short of mesmerizing. The grand jury found Little Lem as "not having the fear of God before his eyes but being moved and seduced by the instigation of the Devil on the fourth day of November AD . . . with force and arms . . . upon one WS Batchelor in the peace of God and the State then & there being feloniously willfully and of his malice aforethought did make an assault."

Rackley pled not guilty to felony murder. He was refused bail, not only because of the prospect that he might flee but also because of the uproar in town and the rumblings that a lynch mob had plans to settle the case early and save officials the trouble of a trial. Rackley's family considered the details of the case and wasted no time in hiring one of the most notable attorneys in the area, prominent Confederate veteran and former Rocky Mount mayor B. H. Bunn. Despite the fact that Bunn had served in the Forty-Seventh North Carolina with Wright, the Rackleys chose him anyway. Bunn quickly made a motion to have the trial continued to the spring session of 1887, and it was granted.

One local paper reported the incident this way: "At Nashville, last Thursday evening, in a difficulty which grew out of a dispute over the killing of a common 'yaller dog,' Lem Rackley, Jr., shot and killed Wright S. Batchelor, the superintendent of the county poor house. Rackley, who is a young man, of about 22, was captured and is now in jail. From a postal we learn that public sentiment is against Rackley."[3]

The news was reported all over the region. In Scotland Neck, a town forty miles north of Nashville, the item read, "Wright Batchelor, a very highly esteemed and clever man of Nashville, NC, was shot and killed by Lem Rackley, Thursday, Nov. 4." The Goldsboro paper referred to Wright Stephen as " a very honorable and clever man," and the *Weekly State Chronicle* in Raleigh used almost identical phrasing. Both confirmed the altercation was about a dog. (Note that the use of the word "clever" in that era was a compliment, much as an obituary today might regard a respected citizen who passed away as "intelligent" or "hardworking.")

Bunn knew the gunning down of a well-respected citizen and government official, with half a dozen witnesses of note, would be a hard case to win. Many still called him Captain Bunn, a moniker he carried the rest of his life after the war. Bunn was no legal lightweight. He had obtained his law license right after the war in 1866 and opened a practice in Rocky Mount. In 1867 he was elected as Rocky Mount's first mayor, shortly after the city was incorporated, and was later appointed by Governor Holden to serve another term, despite being a loyal Democrat. He was the city's attorney for years and Nash County's for three decades. In 1882 he was elected to the North Carolina House and was well known for his knowledge of the law and for his oratorical skills.

Bunn started pulling levers that would eventually lead to a good many controversies in the case. The threats on the life of Rackley continued through the winter, and Bunn appeared in court at the beginning of the spring term to plead for a transfer of the case, telling Judge James Merrimon that it was "unsafe" to keep Rackley in the Nash County jail, and that the young man could not have a fair trial without a relocation of the proceedings. Merrimon was a veteran of the Sixty-Fifth North Carolina Cavalry and the brother of Judge Augustus Merrimon, who once ran for governor and who was a North Carolina Supreme Court justice, U.S. senator, and "bitter Democrat partisan."[4] Judge Merrimon agreed with Bunn's argument and ordered Sheriff Arrington to deliver Rackley to Wilson, a town twenty miles south in the neighboring county of the same name, until the case could be heard, again with no bail being permitted. The transcripts succinctly described the situation: " affidavits having been filed setting forth particularly and in detail facts that show that there are probably grounds to believe that Justice cannot be obtained in this County." The case was moved to the Superior Court of Wilson County. Bunn moved to add Wilson attorneys J. E. and F. A. Woodard to Rackley's defense team. Worthington brought in I. A. Sugg of Pitt County to assist in the prosecution.[5]

Wilson County Superior Court was gaveled in session at 2 p.m. on June 9, 1887, when Wilson sheriff J. W. Crowell brought Rackley in to have the indictment read. Clerk of Superior Court A. B. Deans reported that Worthington moved for a writ of venire facias issued by Sheriff Crowell to assemble a jury—125 men would be called to try and fill the slots. The trial was much anticipated in the eastern part of the state, being noted in the *Raleigh News and Observer* and the *Wilson Mirror* in their Thursday, June 9, editions. The case got mention in the *Wilmington Morning Star* in May, as well as the *Wilson Advance*. There was even "fake news," as far away as the *Weekly Sentinel* in Winston (now Winston-Salem), which reported "Wright Batchelor shot and killed L. D. Rackley, Jr., in Nash County a short time ago." It also mentioned another notable murder case, that of social elite Dr. T. C. Powell of Rocky Mount shooting and killing William Sharp, "a young white man" and the son of representative-elect John J. Sharpe. The Powell case was quite scandalous and pulled some of the public attention away from the Batchelor murder.

The scrolls were brought into the court, and Register of Deeds B. J. Barnes as well as Sheriff Crowell and Deputy Sheriff W. P. Snakenberg pulled and notified the men who would serve on the jury. The jury was seated, and the trial began on June 10.

This is where details become sketchy. At 9 a.m. on Saturday morning, June 11, 1887, after just one day of testimony, evidence, and deliberation, the jury reached a verdict. Despite Rackley being seen by many in broad daylight, on Main Street in front of the busiest building in Nashville, pull a pistol and shoot and kill a Confederate veteran and superintendent of the Nash County Poor House, he was found not guilty of felonious murder. He was instead found guilty of the lesser crime of felonious slaying, "the killing of [a] human being without justification or excuse" and sentenced to three years of hard labor in state prison. The trial and sentence had been a sham.

The public was again stirred, evidenced by coverage in the *Franklin Times* in nearby Louisburg, which reported a late plea bargain that does not show up in the surviving records. "*The Wilson Mirror* says that a large number of citizens of that section are indignant at the short sentence of Rackley, the man who was tried there last week for killing Wright Batchelor in Nash County some time ago. He was allowed to plead guilty of Manslaughter, and Judge Merrimon sentenced him to the penitentiary for 3 years."[6]

This is where a lot of speculation and questions come into play. Did the defense attorney, a former officer in Wright's unit, not have any issue with defending someone who shot and killed one of the men in his former unit? Was there resentment at play over Batchelor's choice to survive by jumping at the chance to leave Point Lookout as a Union soldier? Was the outcome influenced by his political views, the fact that as a "common white" his interests in the world did not align with wealthy Democrats who had no intention of allowing equal rights for former slaves? Big Lem could afford Bunn's fees, but he was not wealthy, as the 1880 census lists him as having $3,000 in real property and $1,900 in personal property.

Why was there a plea bargain in such an open-and-shut case? How about Judge Merrimon's sentence of a mere three years in prison for gunning a man down in the street? It is unfathomable that in a time where men could hang for stealing a horse or any number of other lesser crimes that Rackley would escape the noose. How much did politics play in the case? Merrimon and Bunn were hardline Democrats who had no use for the Radical Republicans and scalawags, or their ideas. Was Wright's loyalty questioned, much like the Confederacy had questioned his state's loyalty, because he'd managed to escape the war without a wound? Did his survival instincts during the war harm his prospects afterward, as he'd feared it might when he chose to return to Virginia and fight an unwinnable battle? There are no transcripts of the trial or surviving media coverage of what was said in the courtroom, so there is no way to look back and know. There is no doubt more to the story than recorded history has left behind.

Sally Ann was left to raise her family on her own, and the children were left without a father and their primary means of support. She never learned to read or write, and now there were children to raise and a farm to manage, just as she had during the war, but she was approaching sixty, no longer a young woman. She never remarried and never truly recovered. There was no life insurance, only hard work and uncertainty, and a dependence on her children to carry her through old age, which she managed, eventually applying for a widow's pension.

Wright's end of life was ironic but maybe not all that surprising once he figured out who he was. Like his state, he lost everything in the end because of a war that should never have been fought, trying to make a choice where no good one existed.

1. Portrait of Wright Stephen Batchelor in his Confederate uniform.
Courtesy of Barbara J. Batchelor.

2. "Confederate Monument, Riverside Park, Rocky Mount, N.C." Durwood
Barbour Collection of North Carolina Postcards (P077), North Carolina Collection,
University of North Carolina Library at Chapel Hill.

3. *Burning the Rappahannock Railway bridge. Oct. 13th 1863.* Alfred R. Waud, artist.
Courtesy of the Library of Congress Prints and Photographs Division.

4. Zebulon B. Vance, 1859. Julian Vannerson, photographer.
Courtesy of the Library of Congress Prints and Photographs Division.

5. *Picketts charge on the Union centre at the grove of trees about 3 PM.* c. 1880.
Edwin Forbes, artist. Courtesy of the Library of Congress Prints and
Photographs Division.

6. *Point Lookout, Md. View of Hammond Genl. Hospital & U.S. genl. depot for prisoners of war.* 1864. George Everett, publisher. Courtesy of the Library of Congress Geography and Map Division.

Rocky Mount Mills, Rocky Mount, N. C.

7. "Rocky Mount Mills, Rocky Mount, N.C." Durwood Barbour Collection of North Carolina Postcards (P077), North Carolina Collection, University of North Carolina Library at Chapel Hil

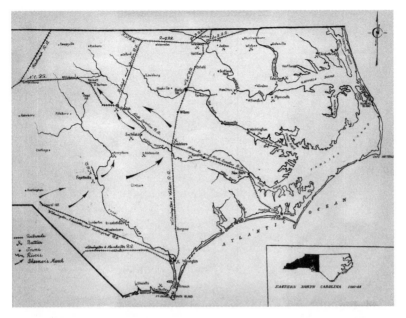

8. Eastern North Carolina, 1860–65. Digital Collection, North Carolina Maps, North Carolina State Office of Archives and History. Courtesy of the State Archives of North Carolina.

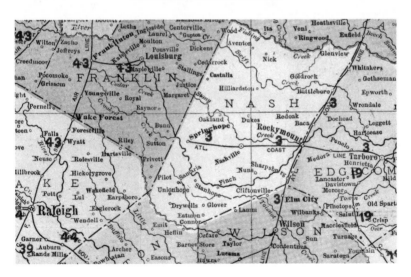

9. North Carolina, 1905. Rand McNally and Company. Courtesy of the Library of Congress Geography and Map Division.

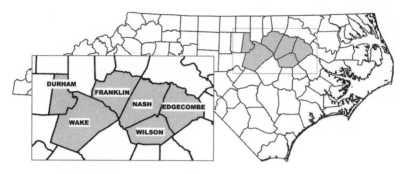

10. North Carolina with counties Durham, Wake, Franklin, Nash, Wilson, and Edgecombe.

11. Nash County Courthouse. Courtesy of Keith Vincent and courthousehistory.com.

Left card:

(B) 1 | U.S. Vols.

Wright S. Batchelder

Pvt., Co. F., 1 Reg't U. S Vol. Inf.

Appears on

Company Muster Roll

for _Sept & Oct_, 1864.

Present or absent ....

Stoppage, $.........100 for.............................

Due Gov't $.........100 for..............................

Remarks: Deserted Sept 14th 1864 at Camp Reno Milwaukee Wis Due the US for (1) one Enfield Rifle and one set of e- quipments complete (1) one Knapsack (1) one haversack (1) one canteen (1) pr. int. scales (1) one bugle (1) one eagle (1) one letter "F" (1) one big "I" (1) one pr Knapsack straps $28.02

Book mark: ....

Hunter

(358)   Copyist

Right card:

(B) 1 | U. S. Vols.

W. S. Bachelor

Priv., Co. F., 1. Reg't U. S. Vols.

Appears on

Descriptive List of Deserters

dated Fort Pier DT April 1865.

Age 36 years; height, 5 feet 7 inches.

Complexion Dark; eyes Dark; hair Black

Where born Nash a N.C.

Occupation Far

When enlisted February 24, 1864;

Where enlisted St Louis Mo

When mustered in Mar 2, 1864;

Where mustered in Norfolk Va

For what period mustered in three years.

When deserted September 15, 1864.

Where deserted Milwaukee Wis

When apprehended ....186 .

Where apprehended...........................

Remarks: ....

Book mark: ....

Springfield

(358)   Copyist

12 & 13 (next page). Wright Batchelor's Union service records. National Archives.

Left Card

B | | **U.S. Vols.**

Wright S. Batchelor

Appears with rank of _____ Pvt _____ on

Muster and Descriptive Roll of a Detachment of U. S. Vols. forwarded

for the ___1___ Reg't U. S. Volunteers.   Roll dated

Norfolk Va _May_ 1, 1864.

Where born _____ _North Ca._ _____

Age _26_ y'rs; occupation _____ _Farmer_ _____

When enlisted _____ _Feb 24_, 1864.

Where enlisted _____ _Pt Lookout Md_ _____

For what period enlisted _____ 3 _____ years.

Eyes _____ _Dark_ _____; hair _black_

Complexion _____ _Dark_ _____; height _5_ ft. _7_ in.

When mustered in _____ _May_ 1, 1864.

Where mustered in _____ _Norfolk Va_ _____

Bounty paid $ _____ 100; due $ _____ 100

Where credited _____

Company to which assigned _____

Remarks : _____

_____

_____

_____

_____

Book mark : _____

(339)   _Copyist._

Right Card

B | | **U.S. Vols.**

Wright S. Batchelor

_____, Co. _G_, _1_ Reg't U. S. Vol. Inf.

Appears on

Company Descriptive Book

of the organization named above.

DESCRIPTION.

Age _26_ years; height _5_ feet _7_ inches.

Complexion _Dark_

Eyes _Dark_; hair _black_

Where born _Tark N.C._

Occupation _Farmer_

ENLISTMENT.

When _____ _Feb 24_ _____, 186_

Where _Point Lookout Md._

By whom _Lt N Harriman_, term _3_ y'rs.

Remarks : _Deserted Milwaukee_

Wis. Sept 14th

_____

_____

_____

_____

_____

(883g)   _Copyist._

12

On the Research Trail

One problem with delaying your start until the research is all
done is that the research is never all done.

—James Alexander Thom, author

School was just out for the summer when I brought up the possibility of a field trip to my always enthusiastic, adventure-seeking, then-fifteen-year-old daughter, Holly. The summer heat was coming on, and I'd just finished my last graduate degree, had a health scare that had hospitalized me for a week, and completed my first year in a new job as an English professor. My interest in Wright Batchelor had blossomed from an essay assignment to a book idea, if only I could get back on track and find some information.

"Holly, I'm thinking of going to the state archives in Raleigh to try to find some of your ancestors," I said one afternoon, after having mentioned to my wife that I was getting back on the project.

"Oh, can I go?" she replied.

I was surprised, considering Holly liked to sleep in on her summer mornings and didn't seem particularly keen on my work. "Absolutely. That would be awesome."

"Good, 'cause Mama told me you were going to need some supervision. I can drive if you pass out or something."

I'd been in the hospital with sepsis and was still weak, but I was anxious to return to the project. My first book, *Memory Cards*, a memoir about growing up in eastern North Carolina, was just out, and I wanted to expand on the story of Wright, which was originally going to be a chapter in that book, but I could not find enough information to finish it on time. Every time I thought his trail had gone cold, I'd stumble over a sliver of another detail, or a book, or my wife would find a newspaper clipping in the course of her nonrelated research projects. It was kind of like golf: enough bad rounds can lead one to consider quitting, but one good shot can wipe all that out (although it should be noted I gave up golf years ago).

The North Carolina State Archives are located in Raleigh, one of the most underrated great cities in America. The assortment of government buildings offer a hodge-podge of architectural styles, but they are clustered together. The archives' boxes and shelves hold one treasure after another for history nerds like me.

The folks who run the security there perhaps should be in charge of more things in our world. Holly and I had to check in downstairs at the security desk and present identification before heading to the elevator. Once we arrived at the first room, a woman in a glass office with a security window passed papers for us to sign, and we had to leave pens, notebooks, and brief cases in a locker—we were allowed only loose paper and pencils inside the large research room filled with tables and chairs; book shelves and card catalogs trimmed the outside walls all around. Any documents had to be requested at yet another desk by filling out a form and having an employee retrieve the box or book. Research is not conducted quickly.

However, after all those steps are taken, a researcher can be handed original materials that are 150 or more years old. It is a unique experience putting one's hands directly onto original documents. I considered that other than the bookbinders, it was very likely that most of the items Holly and I searched through that day had not been touched by anyone in probably a hundred years. After all, we were not in the high-demand section of the papers of former governors, celebrities, or writers; we were digging through pieces of paper from a rural, poor county, a place a researcher would have to be looking for to find, as the old expression goes.

Librarians and the internet and historians and writers have spoiled us as a people. They've made it so easy to look up something. But what I was after was minutiae, from everyday life of everyday people. Most of the "good stuff" is not online, and more often than not it hasn't been digitized. More than once, especially when I was at the state archives and later at the Southern Historical Collection and other rooms at the University of North Carolina, I faced questions about history I perhaps had never considered before: What have we left behind in history? What has been overlooked or forgotten? At 100 years or 150 years or 50 years ago, how easy was it to forget? It seems in school and in my later readings, I, like most people, focused on the stories of the famous, told by their admirers or detractors many generations after their passing. These figures were important, of course, but I admit that like most people, I perhaps overlooked how the decisions and actions of a few affected the many.

Holly and I were fascinated at what we found, and a planned two-hour visit turned into having to be shepherded out the door at closing by state employees, who were simply at work and ready to go home, not two wide-eyed time travelers not knowing what lay ahead on the brittle, stained, browned pages and scraps of paper.

As a matter of fact, the biggest hurdle at the time was trying to find the results of a trial in 1887. I am not a pro at research, not like true historians such as my wife. First, I found out the reason the trail kept going cold was because I had inaccurate information about a trial that took place twenty years after the Civil War: various newspapers reported that it took place in different counties—Nash, Edgecombe, and Wilson. This trip was significant because we found the original handwritten transcripts from the trial. While this sounds as though it would be easy, the pages were bound together by a "general" timeline and not in an exact order. They were also handwritten, and while the script was quite meticulous and in English, it took some time to translate what we were reading and the sometimes misspelled words, or the variation in name spellings and abbreviations. As one might expect, many legal terms have changed in the last century and a half, just as morals and standards have, and in this case few details were recorded. Exact words of testimony were not recorded, and neither was there a summary. The charges of the prosecutor were laid out but not the words from the defense attorney. Photocopies were not practical due to the size of the books, so for the first time in any research project for me, I used my iPhone as a copier and realized what a tremendous short-cut this device offered.

Many arrest warrants and official items were written on scraps of paper and what sometimes appeared to be grocery bags. It was as if a clerk had written "Go arrest John Doe" on a nineteenth-century Post-It note and had passed it to a sheriff's deputy. The informality of official papers was staggering.

There wasn't much order to the court records, and Holly quickly got distracted with the countless pages of assault cases brought against some of our less, uh, civil ancestors. Long ago my wife and I had compiled thorough genealogies of the Brantleys with the help of a local expert and retired schoolteacher, and we recognized many names in the interspersed court records. There was a fornication case against the patriarch and matriarch of the Brantley family, which is another story for another time (a neighbor ratted them out). There were incidents of assault, assault and battery, and a bizarre episode where a neighbor cut out the tongue of one of my ancestor's cows because it was mooing during the night and was apparently worse than a barking dog. Upon discovery, the ancestor knocked on the neighbor's door the next day and promptly shot the animal abuser dead in the threshold of his home before fleeing to Alabama.

We battled to stay focused, and a sweet volunteer who spent a career at the archives and had retired helped us find Confederate pension records, as well as explanations for some legal terms we did not recognize. She was a treasure, and I feel badly that I misplaced her name and couldn't include it here. I never did see her again.

The Raleigh trip offered enough information to keep going. Once we discovered that Wilson, a town within twenty miles of Nash-ville, was where the trial was held, I went to the public library there next. It is a beautiful Georgian Revival–style building built in 1939 that includes a genealogy room with extensive resources, including years of *Confederate Veteran*, a magazine that is an essential histori-cal resource about the Civil War. *Confederate Veteran*, which operated for years on a subscription basis, allowed a forum for veterans, relatives, and descendants to share stories and experiences and helped organize reunions that often included Union veterans. While at the Wilson library, I found a copy of T. E. Ricks's *By Faith and Heritage Are We Joined*, a book locally printed in 1976 that offered a history of Nash County and Rocky Mount, with particularly compelling accounts of the raid on Rocky Mount and other stories. I was later able to purchase a copy on eBay, as it is long out of print and hard to find.

This trip prompted many returns to my "home library" of Braswell Memorial in Rocky Mount. My librarian friend Traci herded me through several resources, including a typewritten copy of the limited surviving records of the Nash County Poor House from the mid-nineteenth century and family books on the Batchelor family and several other families whose names appear in this work. This is where my "history snobbery" was checked. Before this project I was guilty of not paying much attention—and thereby respect—to those who compile and pay to have printed genealogies. Perhaps the stigma is that some feel these projects are egotistical or driven to draw recognition to families. While this could be true, the volumes I encountered at Braswell were accurate and included details that led me to other discoveries or confirmed previous ones. Genealogists do valuable and significant work.

I used the interlibrary loan system extensively for obscure books, and the good folks in the library at North Carolina Wesleyan College were quite accommodating. Sometimes digging through two or three books might only yield a quarter page of notes. That's where my perseverance to follow a good story was tested.

Another valuable pickup was a book on Point Lookout, the prisoner-of-war camp in Maryland. I'd been unable to find exactly what I'd wanted on camp life, and Tom Broadfoot told me about the book, yet another volume long out of print, from which he acquired photocopies from time to time. Braswell has it, and it was invaluable. I returned many times.

It was around this point that I got sidetracked again. The hospital stay for sepsis, my first-ever serious health threat, led to the discovery of liver disease. After the summer ended, my diagnosis went from treating a condition to developing cirrhosis to desperately needing a liver transplant, all in the course of seven months. There were countless tests, and the research and writing had to be set aside for nearly eighteen months.

The year before getting sick, I taught at a small junior college in a nearby county. The library was converting to a mostly digital format and was offering hundreds (if not thousands) of volumes to faculty, students, and visitors, free for the taking. For a book junkie, these were heady times, and I tremendously expanded our home book collection. Among those were several Civil War volumes, including a very handy roster of the soldiers who were at Appomattox Courthouse for the surrender.

As I searched for insight about how life was in antebellum times, I found some great resources, including Joe E. Mobley's *The Way We Lived in North Carolina* in the library at Wesleyan and a copy of Earl J. Hess's *Lee's Tar Heels* at Broadfoot. I met and became friends with the father of one of my daughter's friends, who, as it turned out, is a descendant of Capt. John Thorp. A couple of the books and resources led me to visit Wilson Library at the University of North Carolina—twice. Those digs into the vast expanse of the Southern Historical Collection yielded John Wesley Bone's helpful memoir and filled in small gaps.

A cycle of visiting these places as well as newspapers.com resulted it breakthroughs and frustrations. It is amazing how many newspaper records have survived, but it's sad at how many are lost forever, especially the few papers that came and went over time in Nash County. There is virtually no record of the trial to be found.

I mistakenly thought a search for election records would be easy. A call to the local election board only got puzzled responses from officials. It was as if they thought it unusual that I'd call the Board of Elections for historical election results. Not much turned up on lists in Raleigh either, and again I was alarmed at how quickly and easily it would be to erase history. I was able to find national election results for Nash County from the 1880s, but archives officials and the catalogs indicated there were no local results. However, after digging through a lot of blank pages, I found those missing results and exactly what I was looking for—it would have been easy to miss them, and if I hadn't been obsessed with that piece of the puzzle, I would have missed them (I did inform the archives staff). The archives also published an amazing book of maps and stories about the Civil War in North Carolina. John Gilchrist Barrett's *North Carolina as a Civil War Battleground* was a tremendous help with its statistics and details that I had not seen before.

Other names crossed my path, such as a third great-grandfather on the Brantley side who was an officer in the Home Guard and a trio of ancestors who served in the same company as Wright Batchelor, never knowing that just a couple of generations later the families would be joined. Three other Brantley ancestors died in the war, but none served in the Forty-Seventh.

I was also surprised at the number of mistakes I found not just in newspaper reports but in research, including errors in text that were contradictory to photographs or other physical, documented evidence, including names of families, dates of events, and dates of births. Some caused great complications and distraction, as one implied that a character in this book had obviously had an affair or indiscretion (a pregnancy while the husband was away at war); further research corrected it. Again my assumptions on the inerrancy of public records and publications were put to the test.

At some point, I started referring to Wright as the Forrest Gump of his time. He was part of so much history, while at the same time it passed right through him.

By the time the research was done—which, honestly, continued until the last few words of the book were written—I'd reached many conclusions:

1. There is a lot of work in genealogy.

2. Accurate records are a relatively new thing and shouldn't be taken for granted.

3. You can never assume what you read in a newspaper account is accurate.

4. People really should protect history and family legacies by keeping journals and diaries or some record for their descendants.

I don't know if we think people will always remember or that, in general, what people do isn't significant enough to remember. I don't like either scenario.

5. The lives of ordinary citizens can be at least as interesting as those of "famous" people in history. It is certainly more relatable and, I think, a way to make history in general more relevant and interesting to the general population.

It's not particularly hard to research family history, but it is time-consuming and at times tedious. The internet, with National Park sites, ancestry.com, and other state and national resources, offers a great start—but it's just that, a start. The many people who worked on Civil War rosters have done an amazing job of preserving history, even though their efforts may be often overlooked. Family photos are priceless and make history personal and alive—people should do more than just post these photos to social media; they should make sure these photos are preserved for future generations.

Chasing the trail of Wright Batchelor could have continued well past my stopping point. There's always that temptation to look for one more source . . . but that's the great thing about history and the terrible thing about history. It continues to intrigue and educate and provoke thought long after it is made.

13

Statues of Limitations

[The Southern] memorial movement . . . helped the South
assimilate the fact of defeat without repudiating the defeated.

—GAINES FOSTER, author

We're being insulted and our families are being insulted.
Symbols mean different things to different people in different
contexts. . . . And I don't care what color you are, I've never met
a human being yet who couldn't tell the difference between a
bunch of deranged racists in a pasture dressed up in sheets
and burning crosses and being hateful, and say,
The Dukes of Hazzard.

—BEN JONES to the *Richmond Times Dispatch,* 2015

Confederate statues and memorials are just like every other issue
related to the Civil War—extraordinarily complex and complicated,
with no clear-cut answer as to how to deal with them or even what
they are and what they represent. Basically it depends on whom you
ask and when you ask them. And just like everything else regarding the Civil War, context is essential.

There are 109 Civil War monuments in North Carolina, erected
over a roughly one-hundred-year period from the 1860s to 1961.
The first, "In Memory of the Confederate Dead," was created in
Cumberland County in 1868 and was placed in Cross Creek Cemetery in Fayetteville.[1] In addition to monuments in all the states of

the Confederacy and some of the border states, there are twenty-two states with Union monuments.

A casualty of the media coverage of monument controversy in the country has been context. After the war there was the problem of what to do with the Confederate dead: whether or not they should be returned from the battlefields to their home counties. Congress prohibited the use of public funds to preserve, protect, or identify fallen Confederates.

A year after the war, Decoration Day was organized by a group of women to honor the Confederate dead, but the next year, when Reconstruction became harsher, the federal government took things to another level—women in Raleigh were told they would be fired upon if they held any public processions.

In Raleigh in 1867, federal authorities seized Rock Quarry Cemetery, declared it a national cemetery, and ordered the expulsion of any buried Confederate dead—literally meaning that bodies had to be dug out of their graves and moved. The government refused to provide any assistance regarding the dead, and by doing this united the people of the region to try to come up with some way to memorialize their loved ones.[2]

Like most of the war-torn South, North Carolina was economically devastated. An extremely poor state before the conflict, the state was in even worse shape after it. Since there were very few battles that took place in the state, there were few battlefields to commemorate and only one large one, Bentonville. Because the Confederacy had clearly been mistrustful in its handling of North Carolina officers, there were no great generals to honor. As a result, most North Carolina monuments were not erected to specific people or events but as memorials.

Because of the state ban on using public monies, white women in the South started forming Ladies Memorial Associations (LMAS) to honor the husbands, fathers, sons, and brothers who served or died in the war. While there is no apparent reason for this, most of the monuments in the western part of the state honor all Confederates, while most of those in the east honor the Confederate dead.[3]

After the Fayetteville monument, others popped up in Raleigh, Hoke County, and Wilmington in 1870 and Averasboro in 1872, but the real push didn't start until 1890, the twenty-fifth anniversary of the end of the war. Those early monuments were also part of memorial parks. Most of the monuments erected in the South and the North were established between 1890 and 1920, especially around the fiftieth anniversary (1915) of the end of the war.[4] This is another place where a casual glance at dates can result in a lack of context. Much public comment has been the hasty generalization that Confederate memorials were put up during the Jim Crow era as symbols of intimidation without considering key time markers for when memorials are often created. To add some perspective, while there may have been some ulterior motives during the Jim Crow era with some statues in some areas, it has to be considered that the time period was fifty to sixty years after the war, when many ex-Confederates were in their last days. Throughout history, such anniversaries are when memorials often appear or get traction.

The first North Carolina monument in a civic space was erected by the Ladies of Washington (NC) in 1888, which raised $2,250 over the better part of a decade to honor a local man, Capt. Thomas Allen, and the Immortal 600, a group of six hundred Confederate prisoners of war who were used as human shields by the Union Army and intentionally starved as retaliation for Confederate treatment of prisoners at the infamous Andersonville POW camp. Forty-six of the men died.[5] The statue was placed near the intersection of Water and Monumental Street but was later moved to Oakdale Cemetery because of street traffic.[6]

The first permanent public space monument went up in 1892 on the courthouse lawn in Concord, which is in Cabarrus County near Charlotte, and was paid for by the Veterans and Patriotic Women of the County. The Bentonville Battlefield in Johnston County got its marker three years later. New Bern erected its statue in 1885 and later added one to honor the North, as did the city of Salisbury, which was home to another notorious POW camp. The first big public spectacle took place in 1895 around the monument erected in Raleigh's Capitol Square on May 20. It is believed thirty thousand people were there for the dedication, and it was built mostly with state money. Gen. Stonewall Jackson's widow and granddaughter were brought in to help with the unveiling, and a number of speakers took to the stand. The comments provide some insight into the thinking of the time regarding both the war and the statues. It was said that statues were moving from "cities of the dead" into "spaces of the living."[7]

One of those speakers in Raleigh was Col. A. M. Waddell, who made himself into somewhat of a celebrity monument-dedicator during that time, and his comments were interesting as well. He said, "The South did not go to war for slavery . . . it was the occasion, not the cause of the war."[8] While race rarely came up in monument campaigns, that did not mean those in attendance were not racists.

While Waddell may have been accurate in his remarks, he was certainly not a public leader for healing or reconciliation. He was a provocative speaker and often ranted in opposition to "Negro domination." His name may seem familiar because he was one of the leaders of the coup d'état in Wilmington in 1898 known as the Wilmington Race Riots. That horrific event resulted in the only known overthrow of a civilian government in the United States, resulted in numerous murders of the black citizenry, and forced many blacks to flee the city for their lives. Waddell had served as a lieutenant colonel in the Forty-First North Carolina and resigned because of poor health. He served as a congressman from 1871 to 1879 and considered himself a "champion of oppressed whites."[9]

Henry Wyatt, the first casualty of the war, has two statues. One is on the village green in his hometown of Tarboro, and the other is at the State Capitol in Raleigh, paid for by the United Daughters of the Confederacy. The Tarboro monument has the odd phrasing of "Defenders of State Serendipity" inscribed.

Two other factors in the 1890s played a role in the drive for monuments. In 1893 publication of the *Confederate Veteran* began, and within two years it had over 150,000 subscribers at $1 per year. The magazine was not anti-Union but offered a way for many former Confederates to connect with old comrades or relate stories and experiences of their wartime service. In addition, the United

Daughters of the Confederacy (UDC) formed chapters all over the South and also opened soldiers' homes. In 1898 they established the Southern Cross of Honor, which is a Maltese cross inscribed with the dates 1861–1865 and *Deo Vindice*, which means "God Our Vindicator."[10] Wrought iron versions of these crosses hang in family cemeteries all over the South, some with the added inscription of "First at Bethel, Farthest at Gettysburg, Last at Appomattox." Several of my ancestors' graves are marked with them.

As should be suspected given the history of North Carolina, not everyone was in agreement to the monument building spree of the 1890s. The *Caucasian*, a newspaper edited by Marion Butler and a voice for North Carolina Fusionists, a combination of poor white farmers, blacks, and Republicans, said that money should be spent on public schools, not monuments. "It is not certain any monuments ought to be built on either side to perpetuate the memories of our un-natural civil war," Butler wrote. "The sooner the rancors and hates of that unhappy struggle are forgotten by both North and South, the better it will be for the whole country." Others, like the North Carolina Monumental Association, argued, "A land without monuments is a land without memories."[11]

Still others took the cause of education in another, dark direction, such as Martha Gielow of Alabama, who pressed for more education funding as Northern philanthropic efforts began to educate blacks in the South. She sent a critical letter to the United Daughters of the Confederacy that read in part: "What good will monuments to our ancestors be if our Southland is to become the land of educated blacks and uneducated whites?"[12]

There is no record of a dedication speech expressing regret for reunification at any of the North Carolina monuments. Many of them featured bands playing "Dixie" but also "America." This doesn't fit the profile of treason or intimidation.

And then there is the case of the statue at the University of North Carolina in Chapel Hill, known as "Silent Sam." This monument features an infantryman at the ready with his rifle, but he is silent because he doesn't carry a cartridge box; there is also the campus folklore that if a virgin walks by, Sam will fire his rifle. Silent Sam was dedicated to the 321 students, alumni, and faculty who died in the war. The statue, dedicated on June 2, 1913, has drawn the attention of activists on and off since the 1960s. It was vandalized several times and torn down by riotous protesters in 2018. The chief controversy revolves around the remarks of one of several speakers at the dedication, Julian Carr.

Carr's speech included the usual commemorative clichés used at such events, and it was nothing out of the ordinary until he suddenly took his oratory off the rails with a "rather personal allusion" that could bring someone to consider whether the man was showing early signs of dementia with this vile spewing: "One hundred yards from where we stand, less than ninety days perhaps after my return from Appomattox, I horse-whipped a Negro wench until her skirts hung in shreds, because upon the streets of this quiet village she had publicly insulted and maligned a Southern lady, and then rushed for protection to these University buildings where was stationed a garrison of 100 Federal soldiers. I performed the pleasing duty in the immediate presence of the entire garrison, and for thirty nights afterwards slept with a double-barrel shot gun under my head."[13]

Carr is a perfect example of how the Civil War and aftermath are so damn tangled that it is difficult to sort through events and feelings. It is impossible to defend the remarks of this man, who was sixty-seven at the time and heading into his last decade of life. It would be easy to mark him a racist, a white supremacist, and move on, as both of those statements would appear to be true based on other words he spoke. But history isn't that simple.

Julian Shakespeare Carr, who bears the town of Carrboro as his namesake, was more than that. He was a key North Carolina industrialist, helping form the Bull Durham tobacco company, and was involved in banking, mills, railroads, utilities, and newspapers. He was known as a significant philanthropist as well, helping UNC, Davidson, Wake Forest, St. Mary's, Elon, Duke, and Greensboro colleges, as well as the Methodist Church.[14] He supported women's suffrage and a number of overseas missions for the church, particularly in China. This white supremacist also helped fund the Training School for Colored People in Augusta, Georgia, and helped John Merrick start his career. Merrick was a former slave who helped establish the North Carolina Mutual Life Insurance Company, one of the most important (and early) black-owned businesses in U.S. history. The narrative on Carr is simply not neat or clean or perfect—like most things in history. UNC history professor Peter A. Coclanis wrote in 2017 in the *Raleigh News and Observer*, quoting author Sister Helen Prejean, "People are more than the worst thing they have done in their lives."[15] How are we to treat these figures?

The last Confederate soldier monument in North Carolina went up in 1959 in Alexander County, and the last pre-centennial monument was erected in 1960 in Jones County.

I've got mixed feelings about statues in general, but none of them are strong, which, as someone fascinated by American history and the Civil War, may be odd. It seems most people take a passionate side on the issue. When I was a child, the only one I saw on a regular basis was a World War I doughboy, rifle in hand, in midtrot, in front of the Nash County courthouse. Most of the other statues I saw were grave markers, but like now, cemeteries were not places where I spent much time or felt at ease.

There is a Civil War statue at Battle Park in Rocky Mount, but it always seemed more like a grave marker as well. It has a generic Confederate at the top, seventy-five feet up, looking toward Gettysburg, as the legend goes, watching for his lost comrades to come home, so many who lost their lives or limbs there. Both the solider and the column are white Georgia marble and cost $15,000 (nearly $275,000 in today's money). It sits on a parcel of land that was donated to the city, so that a privately purchased monument to those men could be put in place. The initials CSA are in bas-relief at the base, along with three rifles.

I don't remember the Rocky Mount statue ever coming up in conversation until 2017, when several cities across the South started removing monuments. I have heard lots of inaccurate history regarding the park and statue such as, "it's there to mark the great battle that took place in some war" or to honor "General Battle, who is at the top" (also not true, but in all fairness, Battle is a common Rocky Mount area name). The monument had four carved figures on a lower level, but two were stolen in the 1970s, and the other two were removed by the city for safekeeping. The statue was funded by Robert Ricks and was given over to the local United Daughters of the Confederacy chapter and, eventually, the city of Rocky Mount. Ricks was a Confederate veteran, wealthy postwar businessman and civic leader in the city, and close friend of Capt. John Thorp of Wright's Company A.

The monument's inscription reads: "To the Confederate soldiers of Nash County who in 1861 in Obedience to the summons of their state freely offered their lives, their fortunes, and their sacred honor on behalf of the cause of constitutional liberty and self government and through four years of war so bore themselves in victory and defeat as to win the plaudits of the world and set an example of exalted and unseen patriotism which will ever be an unfailing inspiration to all future generations of American citizens."

When it was dedicated on May 14, 1917, at what was then called Riverside Park, the band played the "Star Spangled Banner," "America," and "The Bonnie Blue Flag." There was a parade from the Ricks Hotel downtown that involved Boy Scouts, Girl Scouts, a band, and other groups. A further complication of the statue's symbolism took a turn in 1976, when a restoration and rededication took place to make it a monument honoring all Nash and Edgecombe veterans of all wars.[16] Another restoration fund-raising effort was started in 2012, and in 2017 some city council members started calling for the statue to be removed.

Over in neighboring Franklin County, home of more men from the Forty-Seventh North Carolina, in the middle of the street that divides the Louisburg College campus, is another statue that went up in 1914. It is a narrow street, and every so often an errant motorist hits it. Adding to the awkward placement is the fact that Louisburg College's student population is predominantly African American. Until recent years most arguments regarding removal revolved around the monument as a traffic hazard. The campus is on the Civil War Heritage Trail, as Union soldiers camped there in the days after Johnston's surrender in Durham. In recent years a group of professors at the college has started a movement to have the statue relocated to a local cemetery, which has created division and some contentious town meetings.

In late 2017 the city of Memphis, Tennessee, removed a statue of Gen. Nathan Bedford Forrest from public property. The attorney for Martin Luther King's assassin designed the statue.[17] Forrest and his men were responsible for the massacre of Union soldiers, most of whom were black, at Fort Pillow as they tried to surrender. Forrest was one of the first, if not the first, wizards in the Ku Klux Klan. Why would citizens want a statue of this man in any community? But once again, an answer that seems obvious isn't clear. Forrest disbanded the KKK after just one year as Grand Wizard. "In January 1869, faced with an ungovernable membership employing methods that seemed increasingly counterproductive, Forrest issued KKK General Order Number One: 'It is therefore ordered and decreed, that the masks and costumes of this Order be entirely abolished and destroyed.'" In 1874 Forrest "volunteered to help 'exterminate' those men responsible for the continued violence against the blacks." By the end of his life Forrest had made significant changes to his attitude: "in 1875, he advocated for the admission of blacks into law school—and he lived to fully renounce his involvement with the all but vanished Klan."[18] How does this make Forrest any different from other Klan or white supremacist leaders of the twentieth century who changed their stances, such as Senator Robert Byrd of West Virginia, who also was a Klan wizard, or Alabama governor George Wallace, perhaps the most famous segregationist of his time, who later publicly apologized and admitted his stances from the 1960s were wrong?

Many ex-Confederates served the reunited country in public service roles after the war. Some were bad men who tried to strip blacks of all their rights at the first opportunity. Too many people make the argument that the men who served the Confederacy were treasonous traitors, but it is not that simple. All of the Confederate generals who were serving in the U.S. Army resigned their commissions before joining the CSA, which had declared itself an independent nation (even though it was never recognized by the world, or the United States, not to mention the debate on the legality of secession), so the charges of treason become less clear. No one was charged with treason after the war. The Confederacy was not trying to overthrow the U.S. government—it was trying to leave it. Many Confederate officers had exemplary careers in the U.S. military and have forts named for them. Most, but not all, soldiers and citizens had their citizenship and rights restored after the war. Jefferson Davis wanted a court trial because he felt sure he could prove secession was legal, and federal authorities eventually decided it would be better to release him. The U.S. Supreme Court resolved that issue in 1869 in *Texas v. White*, when they ruled that the Constitution did not permit states to leave the Union. At various times, from the presidency of William McKinley to federal legislation in the 1950s, measures were taken to provide for pensions and headstones for all Civil War veterans, regardless of what side they served.

Jim Crow laws were coming onto the books when the majority of Confederate veterans were dying (many married young brides, who as widows continued to collect pensions after the vets' passing). Most of the North Carolina statue push came from the UDC, which is hard to categorize as a hate group. It seems that most of the memorial projects were not designed to intimidate insomuch as their timing coincided with other actions that were designed to deny rights and discriminate.

Stereotyping in most everything is a bad idea. It is difficult to make the case that a statue of General Lee that sits in front of a courthouse is justified, particularly if he is outfitted not in his U.S. Army uniform but in his Confederate one. A more complicated question might be whether a park or street or fort name is appropriate; that is further tangled if that property was donated in honor of someone who served in the Confederacy.

Many African Americans are offended by the statues and consider them symbols of hate and racism and monuments to men who represented those ideals. Many white southerners simply want to honor their ancestors.

In reality, the average Confederate soldier or sailor was not fighting to preserve slavery, and the average Union soldier was not fighting to end slavery. Saying statues are white supremacy symbols is oversimplifying.[19]

While we can't know the hearts of everyone involved in the monument movement, we have to put presentism aside and look at what the people of the time wrote and said. Warren County was home to many prominent North Carolinians in the nineteenth century, and their monument offers such an example. The inscription reads "no greater cause," "no greater land," "our heroes." It is not likely "no greater cause" was the preservation of slavery—it was preservation of home and the South. On the other hand, with so much entanglement, with one not being able to be separated from the other, is the South and the Southern way of living at the time and slavery all the same thing?

Talking about any statue brings up more ethical and moral questions as well. The statues to generals are specific and can be debated on that person's merits and service outside the Confederacy. The monuments erected to honor "all the Confederate dead" are somewhat different—many considered themselves to be defending the state from an invasion. How do we apply judgment? There won't be any memorials left to notable figures if each person honored has to have to have their personal life examined and held to a standard of perfection. Do we exclude all the adulterers, crooks, slave owners, racists, and white supremacists? Does the person have to be perfect, as monuments to the Founding Fathers are now being pulled into the controversy? In the end we have to ask, should the statues exist? And if so, where do they belong?

It is as hard to make a case that the statues to specific men should be on public grounds, such as courthouses. For no matter how good these men might have been, and no matter their thoughts on slavery and their stand to protect their state and their homes, had they succeeded in their mission, had they achieved their goal, the United States would have been splintered, and slavery would have continued for at least several more years. While the case can be made that Confederate monuments may not be symbols of hate or tributes to white supremacy, an equally strong case may be made that they represent an effort that inarguably would have continued to treat a portion of its inhabitants unjustly and wrongly.

In August 2017 a collection of activists from communist-affiliated groups to Antifa pulled down a monument in Durham, hot on the heels of the deadly violence of the Charlottesville, Virginia, protests. No sane person condones what the white supremacists had in mind in Charlottesville. Those people don't support America, and they don't love history or the Confederacy—they want a "pure" white nation, as un-American a notion as one can possibly possess. They can be denounced, and one can still choose not to destroy historic artifacts.

The historian in me would rather see the Confederate monuments moved to historic sites than be destroyed by mobs. This, of course, presents another dilemma, that of giving in to mob rule, even if the mob may have some valid points.

For many North Carolinians, these statues were the first exposure to public art and are certainly artifacts of the past. There may have been some intent and ulterior motives during the time these monuments were built, even if it was an ancillary byproduct, but it is impossible to discern. Perhaps some need to come down, and others need to be moved. Maybe those out of the way in public parks, near graves, like the one in Rocky Mount, need to stay and serve as a reminder of where we've been, not to go there again. Those to figures such as William Quantrill (who terrorized the Midwest) or George Pickett (who ordered hangings of men in New Bern), who could have cases made against them as war criminals, are different matters.

Several cities across the South have removed or are considering removal of statues, but few are making plans to destroy them. In North Carolina, as of 2018, a study was ordered by Governor Roy Cooper to consider moving the Confederate statues on the grounds of the State Capitol to the battlefield at Bentonville. There is the main statue for the Confederate dead, one to Henry Wyatt, and one to the Women of the Confederacy. It is interesting to note that Governor Cooper is also a direct descendant of Wright Stephen Batchelor. State law prohibits the removal of statues without the consent of the legislature, with exemptions allowed that include danger of them being damaged or posing a threat to the public.

The statues have a place—perhaps they are just out of place. They are symbols of mourning, not for that lost war, and certainly not for the Lost Cause, but for the lost life, for the destruction of a country, and for the return of the war to our rhetoric.

14

The Future of the Past

Madam, don't bring up your sons to detest the United States
government. Recollect that we form one country now. Abandon
all these local animosities, and make your sons Americans.

—ROBERT E. LEE, from *The Life and Campaigns of General Lee*
by Edward Lee Childe

I think it is the duty of every citizen, in the present condition
of the Country, to do all in his power to aid in the restoration of
peace and harmony. It is particularly incumbent upon
those charged with the instruction of the young to
set them an example.

—ROBERT E. LEE, from "Honoring Lee Anew" by David Cox

The Civil War, like most things in history, is complex and complicated and can't be broken down simply. Neither can the characters,
be they ardent abolitionists, fire-breathing secessionists, farmers,
politicians, or even slaves. All of the actors were flawed, the times
were flawed—and much different from those today.

The Civil War is still being fought. It has reemerged as a heated
debate in our country's history, a cycle that threatens to tear our country apart, battle lines drawn, rhetoric harsh, and with very little interest in sane discourse. How do most people understand the Civil War,
and how has that changed? Why did it take a hundred years for a sus-
tainable, successful civil rights movement to happen? All at once,

anything and anyone associated with the South, the Confederacy, a statue, or a flag is a racist, and anyone associated with removal of the statues, condemnation of the South or the Confederacy or the flag is a communist or doesn't understand heritage. In a muzzle flash, past indifference to history and symbols has become anger. All at once we are all right and we are all wrong, at the same time.

Perhaps Seaton Gales, Confederate veteran and editor of the *Raleigh Sentinel* newspaper, summed it up best over a hundred years ago when he wrote these words about the defeated Confederate States of America: "whether right or wrong, [the Confederacy] was inexpressibly dear to our hearts."[1] Frederick Douglass also had it right when he said, "The South has suffered to be sure, but she has been the author of her own suffering."[2]

Any examination of the legacy of the Civil War in the South has to begin with the notion of the oft-written-about Lost Cause. This was an idea that "created and romanticized the Old South and Confederate war effort and often distorts history . . . [and] many historians have labeled the Lost Cause as a myth or Legend."[3]

The term "Lost Cause" is often credited to Edward A. Pollard, who was editor of the *Richmond Examiner* newspaper after the Civil War. He published an article in 1866 in which he attempted to justify the Southern rebellion. It was entitled "The Lost Cause: A New Southern History of the War of the Confederates." Confederate general Jubal Early, an early proponent of this idea, attempted to build a legacy on promoting the Lost Cause every time he could get a platform, and he was joined by many other notables, no doubt those who sought office or authority. Irony should not be lost on the words "new Southern history," especially in light of attempts to reconfigure historical events in an advantageous way.

With some variations according to source, there are generally six tenets of the Lost Cause:

1. Secession, not slavery, caused the Civil War.

2. African Americans were "faithful slaves" who were loyal to their masters and unprepared for the responsibilities of freedom.

3. The Confederacy was defeated militarily only because of the Union advantage in men and resources.

4. Confederate soldiers were heroic and saintly.

5. The most saintly of all the Confederate soldiers was Robert E. Lee.

6. Southern women were loyal to the Confederate cause and sanctified by sacrifice of their loved ones.[4]

The myth of the Lost Cause has survived and even thrived at times because most of the tenets are at least partially true—but also provably false. In truth, history does not drop itself into nice, neat columns and categories.

Those who hold fast to the Lost Cause often place states' rights, the constitutionality of secession, and tariffs as causes that are either equal to or ahead of slavery. Northerners and abolitionists are labeled as having provoked the war with slavery as a premise but with their own economic preservation at heart. Proponents of the Lost Cause insist that slavery eventually would have died out.[5] A law was passed that the master owned labor, not the life of the slave—again complicating things—and some in the South tried to use this to justify slavery, saying it was no different than an employee-employer relationship and no different than Northern mill owners and their employees.

There is simply too much evidence to set aside the significance of slavery. Georgia, Mississippi, South Carolina, Texas, and Virginia all produced "Declaration of Causes" documents in addition to their ordinances of secession. Each of these documents specifically mentions slavery as a significant, if not essential, factor in secession. Thomas Settle Jr., a former Democrat who helped start the North Carolina GOP, stated, "The war was commenced to perpetuate slavery."[6] There is just too much evidence to downplay this primary cause. That still doesn't mean that's what the men fought for. Many truly felt they were defending the state, flaws and all, and defending their homes. They were not fighting for slavery, but in a tangled mess, those who sought to defend North Carolina were on the same side as those who wanted to maintain slavery.

Confederate vice president Alexander Stephens gave his infamous "Cornerstone Speech" in Savannah, Georgia, on March 21, 1861, and was deliberate in naming slavery as the key factor, at least from his point of view. Among his remarks were these words:

> The new constitution has put at rest, forever, all the agitating questions relating to our peculiar institution—African slavery as it exists amongst us—the proper status of the Negro in our form of civilization. This was the immediate cause of the late rupture and present revolution.
>
> The prevailing ideas entertained by him [Jefferson] and most of the leading statesmen at the time of the formation of the old constitution, were that the enslavement of the African was in violation of the laws of nature; that it was wrong in principle, socially, morally, and politically.
>
> They rested upon the assumption of the equality of races.
>
> Our new government is founded upon exactly the opposite idea; its foundations are laid, its corner-stone rests upon the great truth, that the Negro is not equal to the white man; that slavery— subordination to the superior race—is his natural and normal condition.
>
> Many governments have been founded upon the principle of the subordination and serfdom of certain classes of the same race; such were and are in violation of the laws of nature. Our system commits no such violation of nature's laws. With us, all of the white race, however high or low, rich or poor, are equal in the eye of the law. Not so with the Negro. Subordination is his place. He, by nature, or by the curse against Canaan, is fitted for that condition which he occupies in our system.[7]

When my wife and I first got married, she taught for a short time at a now defunct private school. One of her courses was history, and in 1991 she had to inform many of her students as to who won the Civil War. The school itself had been founded during the civil rights era when many schools were established so that white students might legally avoid attending desegregated schools with black students. Almost none of her students knew that history either.

So many see the Confederate flags as symbols of racism and bigotry. No doubt, a great many people who display the flag are indeed racists or bigots. Hate groups such as the KKK use the Confederate flags as symbols, along with the American flag and the cross. It is obvious how the flag can offend someone because of this. There are plenty of mean, racist, hate-filled people in the general population.

Almost everyone in my area has ancestors who served in the Civil War. To them the flag is about history and heritage and honoring the dead. These are not people who have ever considered slavery "okay" or thought that slaves were much happier before the war than they were after the war when they were free. To these folks, their great-great-granddaddies fought to keep their homes from being burned down and their wives from being raped, and because they thought it was their duty. The thinking at the time was still regional, a leftover from the Revolution and the War of 1812 (when some northern states considered secession), as many states considered themselves countries and, in the view of many, not necessarily united. People thought of themselves as Virginians or North Carolinians first, not necessarily as Americans first. One Confederate said after the war, "[I] had always loved the Union, but loved my state more."[8] There are few degrees of separation back across these generations, and it is most certainly a southern thing to honor those who have passed. It is easy to see how these people find nothing wrong with the flag.

There are many people who wear Confederate flags on T-shirts or have bumper stickers or even tattoos with these symbols that have become part of pop culture, an emblem of rebellion or defiance to the government, a form of complaint or protest. Technically, the commonly seen flag is a battle flag, not the actual, official flag of the Confederacy. Very many of these people have no knowledge of history or the war and merely embrace these totems as symbols of rebellion, of being independent. I've seen T-shirts that read "The Original Boys in the Hood" and that featured robed cartoon Klansmen, which I suppose was meant as a humorous poke or to mock the 1991 movie *Boyz n the Hood*, for those who find hate groups as sources of comedy. I was once at a music festival in Virginia, and when the band on stage took up the opening notes to "Dixie," many attendees rose to their feet and put their hands over their hearts.

The symbology means different things to different people, and the passions run hot as to heritage or hate. Both can be true. All of the factors mentioned in the Civil War's provocations are true. Everybody is right, and everybody is wrong.

We can't tell people what they can and can't be offended by. And in the South, at least, you can't talk-trash about someone's family. There has to be context. It's 150-plus years later, and as a nation we can't even agree what the Civil War was about or what the people of the time thought.

One fact that can't be disputed is that then, as now, they didn't all think the same way.

The flag issue seems to be a simpler one than that of monuments. Why any state ever thought it was okay to fly a Confederate battle flag over a state or federal building after the war seems to be complete nonsense. The only flags that should be flown on government buildings should be state flags or the Stars and Stripes. There is no "but" or exception. How this is even a question seems to defy common sense. If you want to say there were once two countries, then it would make no more sense to fly the Confederate flag than it would to fly the British, French, Spanish, or Mexican flag. If you want to say the states were in rebellion and there were never two countries, then the flag is a sign of disunity or disruption, and it would certainly be disloyal. Private property, of course, is a different story, as is clothing. You can't legislate good taste, or good sense, although I do think even those who fly Confederate flags in their yards—there are plenty flying within a short drive of my house— know in their hearts that the defeat in the Civil War was the greatest blessing for the people in these United States. Tony Horowitz wrote about many more examples in his very fine book about the Civil War in the modern South, *Confederates in the Attic: Dispatches from the Unfinished South.*

Monuments may be a bit more complex. Memorials are not the same as the flag. A statue in remembrance of the men who died does not seem on its face to be offensive. There were many things that complicated the life and conscience of the people of North Carolina and the South in the 1860s. A law was passed in North Carolina on May 2, 1861, making it illegal for state officers to support the U.S. Constitution. Men who joined the army were literally considered by their immediate governance to be taking up arms against an invader. Like so many wars, it was started by rich men and carried out by poor men. I don't for one minute believe Wright Batchelor enlisted to protect some rich man's slaves, or because he wanted to one day own other men.

Another problem with the Civil War is how history has been weaponized by some politicians and other demagogues, with facts as an afterthought. Too few of our citizens know our nation's history. It is true we don't need statues to teach history, as so many have pointed out, but we don't seem to be teaching the history, either. We know this because of the ridiculous notion of some who have compared Confederates to Nazis, a statement that indicates a complete lack of historical knowledge beyond hot takes or sound bites. No sane person today can condone or justify slavery because it was legal, or thinks it was moral then or wants it to come back. The Civil War was not some beautiful Lost Cause. We lost an entire generation of men who put on uniforms, and a staggering number of civilians and vast amounts of property. Perhaps only our geography and distance from Europe and Europe's dysfunction at the time are all that prevented our nation from being conquered by an outside force. The black condition in America after the Civil War only went from a worse situation to a bad situation. Almost nothing was done the right way in Reconstruction, or on the civil rights front, and every American needs to know that and needs to know that history is not a Disney movie, either, where there are clearly good guys and bad guys, and every person is one or the other and that's that. Our history is imperfect, just as our people are. History does not end.

When discussing the Civil War and its causes, it is disingenuous not to consider what the people of that time thought and said. Captain Thorp said in an interview years after the war that it was a mistake for anyone to think that the war was only about slavery—war would have come regardless. Many, if not a majority, knew slavery was coming to an end in the South, both morally and economically. The average North Carolinian was against the war. No doubt it was a war of power, class, and money. Blacks were freed after the war but were far from equal. Very many of those in favor of ending slavery had no notion of allowing property or voting rights for African Americans. Certainly lost on most Southerners was the immense tragedy of Lincoln's assassination. While the record shows that many in the South rejoiced, it was only the fool who could not see that Lincoln was the South's best hope for recovery. It is an interesting exercise to consider how reconciliation and civil rights might have advanced had the mad man Booth not been successful. It is hard to think the plight of both newly freed blacks and poor whites, especially in eastern North Carolina, would not have been improved had Lincoln finished his term and implemented his plans.

The entire notion of secession seems ridiculous. It is hard to conceive how any politician could have ever doubled down on the prospect. There are states today that still talk about secession. There is a notion in California of independence, and there have been other movements to split the state into several states. Every so often there is talk of Texas seceding, and South Carolina has a group that calls itself the Secession Party. It is as much nonsense today as it was 150 years ago. The notion that a country can be flawed, can have a shameful past but still be redemptive, ought to be a notion shared by its citizens, inasmuch as we'd have those same feelings about a fellow human being. Few countries exist for long without a civil war, and very many are torn asunder permanently because of them. The nation's destiny to save the world in the twentieth century would certainly not have been fulfilled had there been two Americas.

The question now becomes how much longer will we fight the Civil War? The answer is not telling African Americans to "get over it," and the answer is not telling other people that their ancestors were all racists and need to be forgotten or shamed. People, especially in the South, are connected to kinfolk, perhaps especially to those they didn't know, because those folks can be put on a metaphorical pedestal. Descendants of slaves and Confederates need to have a respect for both views, for the difficult positions many people were in from all walks of life.

Maybe the biggest challenge in viewing the Civil War is grappling with the ever-popular trend of "presentism" when talking about it or other historical events. Presentism is the application of contemporary or modern moral judgments or worldviews to judge the people and practices of the past; in other words, holding people from other times up against current times. It is the uncritical adherence to present-day attitudes, especially the tendency to interpret past events in terms of modern values and concepts.[9] Historian Paul Bartow said that the "study of the past should be to enter into conversation with historical figures, understand their world as fully as we can, learn from them, and let them challenge our worldview."[10] Another historian, Herbert Butterfield, said historians "should be a 'recording angel' rather than a hanging judge."[11]

Presentism is full of complexities and contradictions and dangers. It can lead to thinking that if historical figures "come up short," their names should be eradicated from history, or at least from public acknowledgment. In general, people in the 1800s were racist, but even the definition of racism has changed. There is a danger in judging a place, culture, time, and belief system of another time you didn't live in—many honorable people of the past were quite flawed held in today's light. For example, by today's standard, most every white American, in the North or South, would have been a racist or a white supremacist, while abolitionists, and later, Radical Republicans, would not have been considered so in their time. In her essay "Against Presentism," Lynn Hunt summed it up this way: "Presentism at its worst, encourages a kind of moral complacency and self-congratulation . . . interpreting the past in terms of present concerns usually leads us to find ourselves morally superior . . . our forebears constantly fail to measure up to our present-day standards."[12] This has come up in North Carolina with such leaders as former governor Charles B. Aycock, who at the turn of the twentieth century did much to advance public education in the state but who was also known to espouse white supremacist views. His name has been removed from some public buildings.

The Civil War has maintained an important role in southern folklore that has really never waned. While it doesn't align with the Lost Cause, bluegrass music has certainly embraced the conflict and has portrayed it as tragedy. A generation ago The Country Gentlemen recorded "The Legend of the Rebel Soldier," which tells the last moments of a young rebel who is dying in a Union prison and asks the attending "parson" if "my soul will pass through the Southland?" The Infamous Stringdusters, a progressive bluegrass band, offered a tribute to Gettysburg with "Three Days in July," and Balsam Range has "Burning Georgia Down," "From a Georgia Battlefield," and "Marching Home." All of these tunes are the blue in bluegrass, all tragic, no romanticism to be found.

Many Confederates worked to restore the Union as soon as the war was over, and some paid the price among their Southern brethren. For example, Gen. James Longstreet took several federal jobs, was unfairly disparaged for it, and was even disrespected when it came to reunions of old veterans and in written histories. Col. John S. Mosby became friends with Grant and served in several federal government posts as well.

On the other side, Southern generals are often highly regarded, and some names, such as Gen. Stonewall Jackson, are still household names. However, a Southern general who remained loyal to the Union, George Thomas, has not been treated well by history. The Virginian, arguably as good as any field commander who served, is barely known by those with casual knowledge of the war, after he made a difficult choice for which he paid a high price.

The country did come back together, and in the twentieth century it became the first super power and a worldwide force for good. It took time.

Former Confederate general and United Confederate Veterans commander John B. Gordon said in 1887 that he wanted to "see one more war, that we [vets] might march under the Stars & Stripes, shoulder to shoulder against a common foe."

Gordon got his wish in 1898 in the Spanish-American War. In that conflict three ex-Confederate generals put on U.S. uniforms and led troops: Fitzhugh Lee, Joseph Wheeler (Theodore Roosevelt's commander), and Gordon. The national consensus was that the South was again part of the Union, that the United States was once more truly whole. Many captured battle flags from the Civil War were returned to the South after this conflict ended.[13]

The regional frustrations persist. There is a perception that the South is still "rebellious" because it holds onto a reverence for Confederate ancestors. But it is so much more complicated than non-southerners sometimes think or consider. I've never met a man from the Sons of Confederate Veterans who didn't have a love for America, a respect for history, and a belief his ancestors would not take up arms against home or the South. For them, it is not about race, although it clearly is for other people.

I love the South and North Carolina, but I'm also angered at times—especially when people try to use symbols to cover or justify their hate. Shouldn't we learn, isn't that how it is supposed to be? We have to move forward and improve without trying to brush over the past. We should remember that we, too, will be judged one day by our descendants, future generations who will have their own knowledge and expectations.

In 1861 Lincoln was not freeing the slaves when he called for troops and invaded the South; he was restoring the Union by force. Slavery may have been a main cause of the war, but for the majority of soldiers on both sides, it was not the cause they fought for. Defending the South from invasion and protecting their homes, or preservation of the Union, was the cause they fought for. Taxes and tariffs played a role, but there is no doubt slavery was the point of the spear. "States' rights" is a valid argument, but perhaps the most documented or prized states' right was the one to keep other men and women in bondage and servitude.

The rich, aristocratic men who started the war can be held accountable for the sins of slavery; as is usually the case, they weren't the ones who did the dying. It was the biggest waste of life in our history, and it might have ended slavery, but it did not completely free the black man. There is no glory in war—only death, destruction, heartbreak, despair, disappointment, and pain.

Epilogue

How long will it take the calloused hearts of men before
the scars of hatred and cruelty shall be removed?

—CLARENCE DARROW, *Attorney for the Damned:*
Clarence Darrow in the Courtroom

Wright Stephen Batchelor is buried in the German Ward Family Cemetery outside Nashville, North Carolina. The inscription on his gravestone reads: "May the Resurrection find him on the bosom of thy God."

Batchelor, even though he deserted, was officially mustered out of the Union Army on May 10, 1866, at Leavenworth, Kansas. He is considered a U.S. veteran. Even if he had not served in the Union Army, Congress passed a law making all Confederates American veterans.

Sally Ann Ward Batchelor applied for a Confederate pension based on Wright's service. The pension program was modified several times. Pension applications included the name, age at application, place of residence, service information, wounds or disability, name of a witness, date of the application, and verification by an appointed county board.

In 1889 there were four classes of pensions based on disability.

In 1901 the North Carolina General Assembly passed amendments to the 1889 law, requiring that pensioners had to be a state resident for twelve months and disabled for manual labor. A First

Class pension paid $72 a month and was for total disability. A Second Class pension was for those who had lost an arm or leg and paid $60 per month. A Third Class pension was for those who had lost a hand or foot and paid $48 a month. A Fourth Class pension was for the loss of an eye or other miscellaneous losses and paid $30. Widows were eligible for Fourth Class pensions as well.

There were exclusions. Those who had more than $500 worth of property or a public salary of $300 or more were ineligible. "Inmates" of soldiers' homes, deserters, and those receiving other forms of state pensions were not eligible.

Other modifications were made by each session of the General Assembly. The property disqualification was raised to $2,000. If a veteran died after 1899, the widow had to be married to him for ten years to collect. If the widow remarried, she lost her eligibility until or unless she was widowed again; at that point she could reapply.

In 1927 a special Class B pension was created for former slaves who had served as support staff in the Confederate military. In 1958 and 1959 more changes came along, including making federal pensions available for former Confederates, but no "double dipping" was allowed.

Sally Ann's application in 1923, when she was eighty-nine, was signed with an X, so it is believed that she never did learn to read or write. Ruffin's wife, Sallie Ann, applied in 1904.

The pension system ended in 1986 with the death of Harriet Victoria Pittman Stallings of Spring Hope, North Carolina, my hometown. Stallings was the widow of Cyrus Stallings of Spring Hope, who served in the Seventieth North Carolina, Company A, and walked home from Manassas, Virginia, to Spring Hope after the war. Mrs. Stallings collected from 1936 to 1986.

Sally Ann Ward Batchelor died on December 20, 1925. She too is buried in German Ward Cemetery. Her headstone is inscribed: "A Tender Mother and Faithful Friend." There are Wards, Odoms, and Cockrells also buried in the cemetery.

Ruffin Batchelor mourned his brother and continued farming. He died in 1900.

Jordan Batchelor, Wright's second youngest son and my great-grandfather, died in 1937. His obituary in the *Nashville Graphic* noted he was a "beloved citizen" and "prosperous planter." Among the many notables who served as honorary pallbearers was B. H. Bunn, the son of the man who defended his father's convicted murderer in court.

The last of Wright Stephen and Sally Ann's children, Wright Stephen Batchelor Jr., died in Nash County on November 28, 1957.

A. H. Arrington served in the Second Regiment of the North Carolina Volunteers. He was a U.S. congressman and a member of the Confederate Congress. In 1863 he voted to increase soldiers' pay to $15 per month, with an additional $5 per month to cover the "deficiency of rations" and to allow an increase in clothing allowance from $50 a year to $130 year. He died in 1867.

John Wesley Bone's memoir was written in 1904 and published by the Wilson County Public Library in 1978. He was among the last living Nash County Confederate veterans. His family's dry goods store operated in the Sandy Cross community outside Nashville until late in the twentieth century.

Thomas Bragg was a two-term governor of North Carolina who was first elected in 1854. He was born in Warren County, directly northwest of Nash County, a prosperous area in antebellum North Carolina but quite impoverished now. Bragg primarily wanted to increase the number of citizens eligible to vote, desired an improved banking system, and called for infrastructure improvements. He was a states' rights Democrat, publicly quiet on secession, but privately he considered it unwise. He was elected to the Senate in 1859 and served until secession, and he later served as attorney general of the CSA for four months until political bickering in the cabinet forced his resignation. After the war he returned to law practice and worked against his former friend and party member William Woods Holden during successful impeachment proceedings. He died in 1872.

B. H. Bunn became wealthy through his law practice and served as Rocky Mount's attorney for several years and as the Nash County attorney for thirty years. In 1888 he was elected to the U.S. House and was reelected two years later. He served as the Rocky Mount postmaster from 1895 to 1897 and died on August 25, 1907.

John Willis Ellis was a two-term governor of North Carolina who succeeded Thomas Bragg in 1858. Like Bragg, he was interested in improving infrastructure, mainly roads and schools. He was at first opposed to secession but quickly changed his tune when it was politically expedient. He died in July,1861, less than two months after North Carolina seceded, and spent all of his brief second term preparing the state for war. He may be best known for replying to Abraham Lincoln's request for troops by telling the president he would "get no troops from North Carolina."

Governor William Woods Holden was impeached and removed from office in 1871 and was denied the right to hold state office again. He was political editor of the *Washington (DC) Daily Chronicle* but returned to North Carolina as postmaster in 1883. He remained active in Republican politics and continued to write. He died of a stroke in 1889. In 2011 the North Carolina Senate voted 48–0 to pardon Holden.

Gen. William Kirkland, from Hillsborough, North Carolina, was the only former U.S. Marine to serve as a Confederate general. After the war he worked as a commission agent and a postal official. He lived for a time in Savannah, Georgia, and New York City. He died on May 12, 1915, at eighty-two, in the Soldiers' Home in Washington DC.

Robert E. Lee never got the amnesty for which he applied, and he died as a prisoner of war on parole on October 12, 1870.

Gen. William McRae, from Wilmington, North Carolina, died in Georgia on February 11, 1882, at the age of forty-seven. He worked as postal official and had a distinguished career as a railroad super-intendent. He had eight brothers, all of whom served in the army or navy, and one of them remained with the Union.

Gen. James J. Pettigrew has a Sons of Confederate Veterans unit, a state park, and a World War II liberty ship named after him. There was a day of mourning in North Carolina when he died in 1863.

Confederate general Roger Pryor of Virginia, who briefly commanded the Forty-Seventh North Carolina in 1862, moved to New York City after the war and was later a law partner of despised Union general Benjamin Butler. He was often referred to as a Confederate carpetbagger. He was a congressman once before the war and once afterward.

Lemon (or Lemuel) "Big Lem" Rackley enlisted as a private in the Twelfth North Carolina, Company H, at Camp Arrington, Virginia, on April 20, 1862, just two months after the birth of his son, Lemon (or Lemuel) "Little Lem" Tolliver Rackley in February. Big Lem was captured September 19, 1864, near Winchester, Virginia, and sent to Point Lookout Prison, where he was exchanged as a POW on March 15, 1865. He returned to Nash County.

Big Lem died October 21, 1901. Little Lem married twice: the first time to Evelyn, who died in 1898, and the second to Mamie, who died in 1955. He served three years in prison for the murder of Wright Batchelor and returned to Nash County. Little Lem died on June 2, 1923. His little sister, Elizabeth, born in 1855, married one of Wright's cousins, George W. Batchelor.

Col. Robert "Uncle Bob" Ricks funded the memorial in his hometown of Rocky Mount and was a close friend of John Thorp's. After the war he returned to farming and became involved in the Rocky Mount Mills and the Bank of Rocky Mount; he became wealthy, adding the Ricks Hotel and Ricks Tobacco Company to his holdings. He served as a county commissioner and in the state legislature, as well as on the state board of education, and was one of the first trustees of North Carolina State University in Raleigh. He was also the target of a robbery in 1900 that resulted in the murder of a man who looked much like him. Two men were convicted and hanged for the crime, the last public hanging in Nash County. It was said that Ricks became anxious about leaving his house for the rest of his life after the incident. He died in 1920.

Capt. John H. Thorp led a long and distinguished life after his service in the Confederate Army. He studied law after the war, earned his license in 1866, and practiced in Rocky Mount. Thorp married Sallie Eliza Bunn in December 1866, the daughter of Rocky Mount planter William Bennett Bunn. He took up farming in 1875 and became a member of the University of North Carolina Board of Trustees that same year. He later served in the state senate in 1887 and retired in 1900. When he died suddenly on February 2, 1932, at the age of ninety-one, after a brief illness, he was referred to as UNC and Rocky Mount's oldest citizen, and he was "remembered as a kindly, loveable man, friendly to all his acquaintances."[1] He was the last survivor of the Bethel Heroes. Capt. John H. Thorp of the Forty-Seventh North Carolina, Company A, wrote *Nash County Confederate Soldiers* in 1925, a list of all the men from the county who served. Thorp was instrumental, with the backing of Robert Ricks, in the construction of the Confederate memorial in Rocky Mount, North Carolina.

Zebulon Vance, of Buncombe County, practiced law in Charlotte after the war until he was elected to the U.S. Senate in 1870. He was elected governor of North Carolina again in 1876 but only served two years after being appointed to the U.S. Senate to finish the term of A. S. Merrimon (Judge Merrimon's brother) in 1878. He lost an eye in 1889 when his health began to fail, and he died three years later after a stroke. He was a popular figure, and when his funeral train headed west, thousands of people lined the railroad tracks to pay their respects.

Jonathan Worth, of Randolph County, was North Carolina's Civil War treasurer, Reconstruction governor, and a legislator, lawyer, planter, and businessman. Worth wrote the law that established the basic structure of the state's antebellum public school system. Worth was elected governor in the fall of 1865 and reelected in a regular ballot in 1866. He fought the Fourteenth Amendment and the Reconstruction Acts, passed early in 1867, which provided for military rule, a new state constitution, Negro suffrage, and elections to replace the existing government. In June 1868, after these arrangements were carried out, Worth was removed from office. He died the next year.

The Confederate States left the Union and did not return immediately after the end of the war. Technically the states were in limbo for years—not a state, not a territory, just undefined. Many in the North felt the states got off easy, but Reconstruction, deserved or not, was bad for the entire country. The secession and readmission dates are as follows:

South Carolina: December 20, 1860–July 9, 1868
Mississippi: January 9, 1861–February 23, 1870
Florida: January 10, 1861–June 25, 1868
Alabama: January 11, 1861–July 13, 1868
Georgia: January 19, 1861–July 21, 1868; July 15, 1870
    (approval of Fifteenth Amendment)
Louisiana: January 26, 1861–July 9, 1868
Texas: February 1, 1861–March 30, 1870
Virginia: April 17, 1861–January 26, 1870
Arkansas: May 6, 1861–June 22, 1868
North Carolina: May 20, 1861–July 4, 1868
Tennessee: May 7 (declared independence) and June 8
    (voted for independence), 1861–July 24, 1866

There are thirteen stars on the official Confederate flag, even though only eleven states seceded. The last two stars are for Kentucky and Missouri, which had provisional governments for both the Union and the Confederacy, as well as representatives in the U.S. and Confederate Congresses. Both states pledged neutrality. However, when Gen. Leonidas Polk moved troops to Columbus, Kentucky, and Gen. Ulysses S. Grant moved troops to Paducah, Kentucky, it seemed impossible. The legislature had pledged to go with the South if the situation arose, but instead it stayed in the Union on the grounds that the South had violated neutrality first. In Missouri, U.S. forces arrested the Missouri State Guard and declared the state government deposed when the legislature-in-exile seceded.[2] Kentucky supplied about 100,000 men to the Union forces and between 25,000 and 40,000 to the Confederate side. Missouri sent 110,000 to the Union and 30,000 to the Confederacy.

Arizona owes the Confederacy at least partial credit for being able to attain statehood. In 1856 Arizona was part of the New Mexico Territory and petitioned Washington to be separated. Some in Arizona saw the secession of the Southern states as an opportunity. A convention in March 1861 pledged Arizona as a Confederate state, and less than two weeks later the measure was ratified. U.S. troops pulled out, and Confederate lieutenant colonel John Baylor captured Fort Fillmore.

Baylor declared Arizona Confederate territory and appointed himself governor, and by August 1861 Arizona sent a delegate to the Confederate Congress. The Union was not about to let this stand, so in February 1862 President Lincoln established the Territory of Arizona. Statehood took another fifty years, and Arizona became the last of the forty-eight contiguous states.

Also represented in the Confederate Congress was the Indian Territory. A July 1861 treaty with the Choctaw and Chickasaw tribes led to the Five Civilized Nations being represented. In addition, citizens of these nations served in the Confederate Army.

For years, blame for Pickett's/Pettigrew's Charge was argued. Virginia newspapers came to Pickett's defense, while North Carolina papers backed Pettigrew. Perhaps the best work on this topic is *Pickett or Pettigrew*, an essay by W. R. Bond published by the Butternut Press in 1984.

Rocky Mount Mills was rebuilt after the war in 1865 and then was burned down again in 1869 by a disgruntled employee. The mill was rebuilt again and operated until 1996. A major renovation of the property is going on now, after previous starts that faltered. The complex features brew mills, restaurants, and office space and hosts many events in Rocky Mount. Many of the old mill village houses have been refurbished and have been sold or leased. Battle Park is the original site of Rocky Mount Falls and the location of the first post office in Rocky Mount. One of the men in the federal cavalry unit that burned Rocky Mount Mills was Russell Conwell, who went on to be a preacher, author, and founder of Temple University.

The Nash County Poor House remained in operation until 1923, when the county commissioners subdivided the property and sold off large parcels. They built a new facility that year and renamed it the County Home, and today the road that leads by the property near the micro-town of Momeyer is called Old County Home Road. Many of the buildings have been moved and modified but are still standing and in use. The old superintendent's house once occupied by Wright Batchelor is now a private residence.

Wilmer McLean, a farmer and grocer, is famous for having moved from Manassas, where his farm was the scene of a major battle in 1861, to Appomattox, a place he thought would be safe from the war. In perhaps one of the strangest ironies of the war, his properties were essentially the landmark bookends of the war.

Notes

1. Homecoming

1. Moore, Hill, and Bandel, *Old North State at War.*
2. Lindemann, "Aftermath of the Civil War."
3. "American History Series."

2. A Name in a Book

1. *North Carolina Troops.*
2. Powell, *North Carolina Gazetteer.*
3. Rackley, *Minutes of the Wardens of the Poor.*

3. The Rip Van Winkle State

1. Ricks, *By Faith and Heritage.*
2. Ricks, *By Faith and Heritage.*
3. Ricks, *By Faith and Heritage.*
4. Mobley, *Way We Lived.*
5. Mobley, *Way We Lived.*
6. Ricks, *By Faith and Heritage.*
7. "North Carolina's Civil War Story."
8. Moore, Hill, and Bandel, *Old North State at War.*
9. Wiley, *Embattled Confederates,* 185.
10. Ricks, *By Faith and Heritage,* 238.
11. Downs, "Death Knell of Slavery."
12. "North Carolina's Civil War Story."
13. Downs, "Death Knell of Slavery."
14. Moore, Hill, and Bandel, *Old North State at War.*
15. "North Carolina's Civil War Story."
16. Madden, *Beyond the Battlefield.*

4. A New Life

1. Rackley, *Minutes of the Wardens of the Poor.*
2. Rackley, *Minutes of the Wardens of the Poor.*
3. Powell, *North Carolina through Four Centuries.*
4. Turley, "Secession."
5. Powell, *North Carolina through Four Centuries.*
6. Moore, Hill, and Bandel, *Old North State at War.*
7. Pitts, "Bragg, Thomas."
8. Tolbert, "Ellis, John Willis."
9. Powell, *North Carolina through Four Centuries*, 342.
10. Tolbert, "Ellis, John Willis."
11. Moore, Hill, and Bandel, *Old North State at War.*
12. Ricks, *By Faith and Heritage*, 91.
13. Butler, *North Carolina Civil War Monuments*, 74.
14. Madden, *Beyond the Battlefield*, 25.
15. Arrington, "Papers of A. H. Arrington."
16. Arrington, "Papers of A. H. Arrington."
17. "Secession Acts."
18. Larson, "Free and Independent State."
19. Powell, *North Carolina through Four Centuries*, 347–48.
20. Powell, *North Carolina through Four Centuries*, 351.
21. Arrington, "Papers of A. H. Arrington."
22. Arrington, "Papers of A. H. Arrington."
23. Butler, *North Carolina Civil War Monuments.*
24. Boyer et al., *Enduring Vision*, 422.

5. My Civil War Past

1. *Asheville Citizen Times*, September 28, 1922.

6. Wright's Enlistment

1. McKinney, *Zeb Vance.*
2. Thorpe, "John Houston Thorpe Papers."
3. Bone, *Personal Memoir*, 3.
4. Madden, *Beyond the Battlefield.*
5. Bone, *Personal Memoir*, 2.
6. Gerard, "Burden of War."
7. *Semi-Weekly State Journal* (Raleigh NC), April 5, 1862, 3.
8. Clark, *Histories of the Several Regiments*, 86.
9. Bone, *Personal Memoir.*
10. Madden, *Beyond the Battlefield.*
11. Gerard, "James Johnston Pettigrew."

7. Bloodbaths at Gettysburg and Bristoe

1. Hess, *Lee's Tar Heels*, 127.
2. *North Carolina Troops*, 241.
3. *North Carolina Troops*, 241.
4. *North Carolina Troops*, 241.
5. *North Carolina Troops*, 241.
6. Hess, *Lee's Tar Heels*, 137.
7. Clark, *Histories of the Several Regiments*, 90.
8. Hess, *Lee's Tar Heels*, 147.
9. *North Carolina Troops*, 241.
10. Clark, *Histories of the Several Regiments*, 109.
11. "Casualties in North Carolina Troops."
12. *North Carolina Troops*.
13. Gerard, "James Johnston Pettigrew."
14. *North Carolina Troops*, 242.
15. Hess, *Lee's Tar Heels*, 190; Clark, *Histories of the Several Regiments*, 92.
16. Thorpe, "John Houston Thorpe Papers."

8. The Home Front

1. Norris, "Rocky Mount Mills."
2. Norris, "Rocky Mount Mills."
3. Barrett, *Civil War in North Carolina*, 165.
4. Ricks, *By Faith and Heritage*.
5. Moore, Hill, and Bandel, *Old North State at War*, 49; Ricks, *By Faith and Heritage*, 96.
6. Ricks, *By Faith and Heritage*.
7. Ricks, *By Faith and Heritage*.
8. N. Brown, "Union Election," 385.
9. N. Brown, "Union Election," 392.
10. Moore, Hill, and Bandel, *Old North State at War*.
11. Gerard, "Deserters and Outliers."
12. "Peace Party."
13. Butler, *North Carolina Civil War Monuments*, 75.
14. Eicher, "Coming Apart from the Inside."
15. Moore, Hill, and Bandel, *Old North State at War*.
16. Ricks, *By Faith and Heritage*.
17. Gerard, "Deserters and Outliers."
18. McPherson, *Illustrated Battle Cry of Freedom*.
19. McPherson, *Illustrated Battle Cry of Freedom*, 528.
20. Moore, Hill, and Bandel, *Old North State at War*, 64–65.
21. Lerner, "Money, Prices, and Wages."

22. Moore, Hill, and Bandel, *Old North State at War*.

23. Hamblen and Powell, *Connecticut Yankees at Gettysburg*, 110.

24. Moore, Hill, and Bandel, *Old North State at War*, 70.

25. Powell, *North Carolina through Four Centuries*.

26. Clark, *Histories of the Several Regiments*, 2.

27. "Zebulon B. Vance."

9. POW Life

1. "Point Lookout."

2. Hesseltine, *Civil War Prisons*.

3. Beitzell, *Point Lookout Prison Camp*.

4. "Point Lookout."

5. Hesseltine, *Civil War Prisons*.

6. Hesseltine, *Civil War Prisons*.

7. T. Brown, *Dorothea Dix*, 319.

8. This was issued from Chattanooga on December 12, 1863, General Orders, No. 10, by General Grant.

9. D. Brown, *Galvanized Yankees*, 158.

10. Current, *Lincoln's Loyalists*, 242.

11. Civil War Soldiers—Union—CSA.

12. *Appomattox Roster*.

13. Bone, *Personal Memoir*, 21; Clark, *Histories of the Several Regiments*, 98.

14. Kinard, *Battle of the Crater*.

15. Hess, *Lee's Tar Heels*, 290.

16. Clark, *Histories of the Several Regiments*, 100.

17. McPherson, *Illustrated Battle Cry of Freedom*.

18. Clark, *Histories of the Several Regiments*, 100.

19. Watkins, *Co. Aytch*, 46.

20. McPherson, *Illustrated Battle Cry of Freedom*.

21. McPherson, *Illustrated Battle Cry of Freedom*, 746.

22. Thorpe, "John Houston Thorpe Papers."

23. McPherson, *Illustrated Battle Cry of Freedom*, 747.

24. Siegel, *No Backward Step*, 241.

25. McPherson, *Illustrated Battle Cry of Freedom*, 747.

10. Return and Reconstruction

1. Bone, *Personal Memoir*, 36.

2. Bone, *Personal Memoir*, 37.

3. Gerard, "One Nation."

4. Gerard, "One Nation."

5. Gerard, "One Nation."

6. Moore, Hill, and Bandel, *Old North State at War*.

7. Wittenberg, "All or Nothin'."

8. Wittenberg, "All or Nothin'."

9. Wittenberg, "All or Nothin'."

10. Moore, Hill, and Bandel, *Old North State at War*.

11. Powell, "North Carolina through Four Centuries."

12. Powell, "North Carolina through Four Centuries."

13. *North Carolina Troops.*

14. Raper, *Rocky Mount's Confederate Mayors.*

15. Butler, *North Carolina Civil War Monuments.*

16. *Nashville Graphic*, October 18, 1928.

11. Trouble about a "Yaller" Dog

1. Some of the information about the incident comes from the *Wilmington (NC) Morning Star*, November 9, 1886.

2. Nash County Court Records, 1887, North Carolina State Archives.

3. "Crimes and Casualties."

4. "Southern Campaign."

5. "Wilson News."

6. *Franklin Times* (Louisburg NC), June 17, 1887.

13. Statues of Limitations

1. Butler, *North Carolina Civil War Monuments.*

2. Butler, *North Carolina Civil War Monuments.*

3. Butler, *North Carolina Civil War Monuments.*

4. Christensen, "Complex Origins of Confederate Monuments."

5. Butler, *North Carolina Civil War Monuments.*

6. Butler, *North Carolina Civil War Monuments.*

7. Butler, *North Carolina Civil War Monuments*, 41.

8. Butler, *North Carolina Civil War Monuments*, 45.

9. Umfleet, *Day of Blood*, 48.

10. Butler, *North Carolina Civil War Monuments.*

11. Butler, *North Carolina Civil War Monuments*, 46.

12. Butler, *North Carolina Civil War Monuments*, 95.

13. Coclanis, "Julian Carr Did Wrong."

14. Queen, "Carr, Julian Shakespeare."

15. Coclanis, "Julian Carr Did Wrong."

16. "Nash County Confederate Monument."

17. Tures, "General Nathan Bedford Forrest."

18. Tures, "General Nathan Bedford Forrest."

19. Christensen, "Complex Origins of Confederate Monuments."

14. The Future of the Past

1. Butler, *North Carolina Civil War Monuments*, 14.

2. Douglass, "Speech Delivered in Madison Square."

3. Janney, "Lost Cause."

4. Janney, "Lost Cause."

5. Janney, "Lost Cause."

6. Blight, *Race and Reunion*, 48.

7. Stephens, "'Cornerstone' Speech."

8. Butler, *North Carolina Civil War Monuments*, 45.

9. Davenport, "Presentism."

10. Bartow, "Growing Threat of Historical Presentism."

11. Bartow, "Growing Threat of Historical Presentism."

12. Hunt, "Against Presentism."

13. Butler, *North Carolina Civil War Monuments*, 88.

Epilogue

1. Thorpe, "John Houston Thorpe Papers."

2. Cannon, "Why Are There 13 Stars?"

Bibliography

"American History Series: Robert E. Lee's Surrender." Learning English, Voice of America, December 23, 2009. https://learningenglish.voanews.com/a /a-23-2009-12-23-voa1-83141032/115690.html.

The Appomattox Roster. New York: Antiquarian Press, 1962.

Arrington, Archibald Hunter. "A. H. Arrington Papers, 1744–1909." Southern Historical Collection, Wilson Library, University of North Carolina at Chapel Hill.

Barrett, John Gilchrist. *The Civil War in North Carolina.* Chapel Hill: University of North Carolina Press, 1963.

———. *North Carolina as a Civil War Battleground, 1861–1865.* Raleigh NC: State Department of Archives and History, 1960.

Bartow, Paul. "The Growing Threat of Historical Presentism." *AEIdeas*, American Enterprise Institute, Washington DC, December 10, 2015. https://www .aei.org/society-and-culture/the-growing-threat-of-historical-presentism/.

Beitzell, Edwin Warfield. *Point Lookout Prison Camp for Confederates.* Self-published, 1972.

Blaisdell, Robert, ed. *The Civil War: A Book of Quotations.* New York: Dover, 2004.

Blight, David W. *Race and Reunion: The Civil War in American Memory.* Cambridge MA: Belknap Press/Harvard University Press, 2002.

Bone, John Wesley. *A Personal Memoir of the Civil War Service of John Wesley Bone: A Confederate Soldier from Nash County, North Carolina.* Wilson NC: Wilson County Public Library, 1978.

Bowman, John S., ex. ed. *The Civil War Almanac.* New York: Gallery Books, 1983.

Boyer, Paul S., Clifford E. Clark Jr., Karen Halttunen, Joseph F. Kett, Neal Salisbury, Harvard Sitkoff, Nancy Woloch, and Andrew Rieser. *The Enduring Vision: A History of the American People.* 9th ed. Boston: Cengage Learning, 2018.

Brown, Dee. *The Galvanized Yankees.* New York: Open Road Integrated Media, 2012.

Brown, Norman D. "A Union Election in Civil War North Carolina." *North Carolina Historical Review* 43, no. 4 (Autumn 1966): 381–400.

Brown, Thomas J. *Dorothea Dix: New England Reformer*. Cambridge MA: Harvard University Press, 1998.

Butler, Douglas J. *North Carolina Civil War Monuments: An Illustrated History*. Jefferson NC: McFarland, 2013.

Cannon, Devereaux D., Jr. "Why Are There 13 Stars on Confederate Flags?" Confederate Flags. http://confederateflags.org/fotcfaq/fotcfaq4/.

"Casualties in North Carolina Troops." *Raleigh (NC) Register*, July 15, 1863.

Christensen, Rob. "The Complex Origins of Confederate Monuments." *News and Observer* (Raleigh NC), September 22, 2017.

Civil War Soldiers—Union—CSA. Fold3—Military Records. National Archives and Record Administration. fold3/ancestry.com.

Clark, Walter, ed. *Histories of the Several Regiments and Battalions from North Carolina in the Great War, 1861–1865*. Vol. 3. Raleigh: State of North Carolina, 1901.

Coclanis, Peter A. "Julian Carr Did Wrong, but Also a Good Deal Right." *News and Observer* (Raleigh NC), September 26, 2017.

"Crimes and Casualties." *Trees of Wilson*. Wilson NC: Wilson County Genealogical Society, January 2009.

Current, Richard Nelson. *Lincoln's Loyalists: Union Soldiers from the Confederacy*. Boston: Northeastern University Press, 1992.

Davenport, David. "Presentism: The Dangerous Virus Spreading across College Campuses." *Forbes*, December 1, 2015.

Douglass, Frederick. "Speech Delivered in Madison Square, New York, Decoration Day." 1878. Frederick Douglass Papers, Library of Congress. https://www.loc.gov/item/mfd.23011/.

Downs, Gregory P. "The Death Knell of Slavery." *New York Times*, May 19, 2011. https://opinionator.blogs.nytimes.com/2011/05/19/the-death-knell-of-slavery/?_r=0.

Eicher, David J. "Coming Apart from the Inside: How Internal Strife Brought Down the Confederacy." *Civil War Times*, January 2008.

"Elm Grove Church Has Great Days." *Nashville (NC) Graphic*, October 18, 1928.

Faust, Patricia L. *Historical Times Illustrated Encyclopedia of the Civil War*. New York: Harper and Row, 1986.

"From the Forty-Seventh Regiment." *Daily Progress* (New Bern NC), July 14, 1863.

Gerard, Philip. "The Burden of War." *Our State Magazine* (North Carolina), July 31, 2012.

———. "Deserters and Outliers." *Our State Magazine* (North Carolina), January 29, 2014.

———. "James Johnston Pettigrew: A Scholar in the Civil War." *Our State Magazine* (North Carolina), August 5, 2013.

———. "One Nation, Again, After Johnston's Surrender." *Our State Magazine* (North Carolina), April 7, 2015.

Hamblen, Charles P., and Walter L. Powell. *Connecticut Yankees at Gettysburg*. Kent OH: Kent State University Press, 1993.

Hess, Earl J. *Lee's Tar Heels*. Chapel Hill: University of North Carolina Press, 2002.

Hesseltine, William B. *Civil War Prisons: A Study in War Psychology*. Kent OH: Kent State University Press, 1972.

Hunt, Lynn. "Against Presentism." *Perspectives on History*, American Historical Association, May 1, 2002. https://www.historians.org/publications-and -directories/perspectives-on-history/may-2002/against-presentism.

Janney, Caroline E. "The Lost Cause." *Encyclopedia Virginia*, Virginia Foundation for the Humanities, July 27, 2016. https://www.encyclopediavirginia .org/Lost_Cause_The.

Kinard, Jeff. *The Battle of the Crater*. Abilene TX: McWhiney Foundation Press, 1998.

Larson, Jennifer L. "'A Free and Independent State': North Carolina Secedes from the Union." Documenting the American South, University Library, University of North Carolina at Chapel Hill. https://docsouth.unc.edu/highlights /secession.html.

Lerner, Eugene M. "Money, Prices, and Wages in the Confederacy, 1861–1865." *Journal of Political Economy* 63, no. 1 (February 1955): 20–40.

Lindemann, Erika. "Aftermath of the Civil War." Documenting the American South, University Library, University of North Carolina at Chapel Hill. https://docsouth.unc.edu/true/chapter/chp06-02/chp06-02.html.

Madden, David. *Beyond the Battlefield: The Ordinary Life and Extraordinary Times of the Civil War Soldier*. New York: Simon & Schuster, 2000.

McKinney, Gordon. *Zeb Vance: North Carolina's Civil War Governor and Gilded Age Political Leader*. Chapel Hill: University of North Carolina Press, 2004.

McPherson, James M. *The Illustrated Battle Cry of Freedom: The Civil War Era*. New York: Oxford University Press, 2003.

Mobley, Joe A., ed. *The Way We Lived in North Carolina*. Chapel Hill: University of North Carolina Press, 2003.

Moore, Mark A., Michael Hill, and Jessica A. Bandel. *The Old North State at War: The North Carolina Civil War Atlas*. Raleigh: North Carolina Office of Archives and History, 2015.

"Nash County Confederate Monument." Durwood Barbour Collection of North Carolina Postcards (P0077), North Carolina Collection, University of North Carolina Library at Chapel Hill.

Norris, David A. "Rocky Mount Mills." NCpedia, 2006. https://www.ncpedia .org/rocky-mount-mills.

"North Carolina's Civil War Story: The Road to Secession." North Carolina Historic Sites. https://historicsites.nc.gov/resources/north-carolina-civil-war /road-secession.

North Carolina Troops, 1861–1865: A Roster. Vol. 11, *Infantry (45th–48th Regiments)*. Raleigh: North Carolina Office of Archives and History.

"Of the 151 in Co. A. 47th Reg., Nine are Living: Thorpe Tells Fate That Befell His Comrades." *Asheville Citizen Times*, September 28, 1922.

"Peace Party (American Civil War)." North Carolina History Project, 2016. http://northcarolinahistory.org/encyclopedia/peace-party-american-civil-war/.

Pitts, C. E. "Bragg, Thomas." NCpedia, 1979. https://www.ncpedia.org/biography/bragg-thomas.

"Point Lookout." The Prisoners of War, Sons of Confederate Veterans. http://www.wadehamptoncamp.org/hist-p-plo.html.

Powell, William S. *The North Carolina Gazetteer.* Chapel Hill: University of North Carolina Press, 1968.

———. *North Carolina through Four Centuries.* Chapel Hill: University of North Carolina Press, 1989.

Queen, Louise L. "Carr, Julian Shakespeare." NCpedia, 1979. https://www.ncpedia.org/biography/carr-julian-shakespeare.

Rackley, Timothy. *Minutes of the Wardens of the Poor, 1844–1869.* Kernersville NC: T. W. Rackley, 1997. Braswell Memorial Library, Rocky Mount NC.

Raper, Stephen W. *Rocky Mount's Confederate Mayors.* Braswell Memorial Library, Rocky Mount NC.

Ricks, T. E., ed. *By Faith and Heritage Are We Joined: A Compilation of Nash County Historical Notes.* Rocky Mount NC: Nash County Bicentennial Commission, 1976.

Rogers, J. Rowan. "Additional Sketch Forty-Seventh Regiment." In *North Carolina Troops.*

"Secession Acts of the Thirteen Confederate States: North Carolina." American Battlefield Trust. https://www.battlefields.org/learn/primary-sources/secession-acts-thirteen-confederate-states#NORTH_CAROLINA.

Siegel, Charles G. *No Backward Step: A Guide to Grant's Campaign in Virginia.* Shippensburg PA: Burd Street Press, 2000.

"The Southern Campaign." *New York Times,* October 14, 1878.

Stephens, Alexander H. "'Cornerstone' Speech." March 21, 1861. Teaching American History, Ashbrook Center, Ashland University. https://teachingamericanhistory.org/library/document/cornerstone-speech/.

Thorp, John H. "Forty-Seventh Regiment." In *North Carolina Troops.*

Thorpe, John Houston. "John Houston Thorpe Papers, 1861; 1864; 1930; 1932." Southern Historical Collection, Wilson Library, University of North Carolina at Chapel Hill.

Tolbert, Noble J. "Ellis, John Willis." NCpedia, 1986. https://www.ncpedia.org/biography/ellis-john-willis.

Tures, John A. "General Nathan Bedford Forrest versus the Ku Klux Klan." *Huffington Post,* July 6, 2015. https://www.huffpost.com/entry/general-nathan-bedford-fo_b_7734444.

Turley, Jonathan. "Secession." Historynet. http://www.historynet.com/secession.

Umfleet, LeRae Sikes. *A Day of Blood: The 1898 Wilmington Race Riot.* Raleigh: North Carolina Office of Archives and History, 2009.

Watkins, Sam R. *Co. Aytch: A Side Show of the Big Show.* New York: Collier Books, 1962.

Wiley, Bell Irvin. *Embattled Confederates: An Illustrated History of Southerners at War.* New York: Harper and Row, 1964.

Williams, Lyle Keith. *The Batchelor Family.* Wyandotte OK: Gregath, 1995. Braswell Memorial Library, Rocky Mount NC.

Williams, Wiley J. "Rip Van Winkle State." NCpedia, 2006. https://www.ncpedia .org/rip-van-winkle-state.

"Wilson News." *News and Observer* (Raleigh NC), June 14, 1887.

Wittenburg, Eric J. "All or Nothin': The Surrender Sherman and Johnston Crafted at Bennett Place." Historynet, March 2018. http://www.historynet.com/nothin -surrender-bennett-place.htm.

"Zebulon B. Vance: Civil War Governor and Reconstruction Senator." Civil War Experience, North Carolina Department of Cultural Resources/Office of Archives and History. http://civilwarexperience.ncdcr.gov/vance/narrative -vance3.htm (site discontinued).